HARMONY FOR COUPLES

A Divorce Lawyer's Ultimate Guide to
MARRIAGE SUCCESS

JOYCE KHOO

The stories in this book are based on real clients I have represented or couples I have counselled. Names and identifying characteristics have been changed to protect the privacy of these individuals. Before you think about suing me for breaching lawyer-client confidentiality, let me assure you, I haven't.

First published by Ultimate World Publishing 2020
Copyright © 2020 Joyce Khoo

ISBN

Paperback: 978-1-922497-30-7
Ebook: 978-1-922497-31-4

Joyce Khoo has asserted her rights under the Copyright, Designs and Patents Act 1988 to be identified as the author of this work. The information in this book is based on the author's experiences and opinions. The publisher specifically disclaims responsibility for any adverse consequences which may result from use of the information contained herein. Permission to use information has been sought by the author. Any breaches will be rectified in further editions of the book.

All rights reserved. No part of this publication may be reproduced, stored in or introduced into a retrieval system, or transmitted in any form, or by any means (electronic, mechanical, photocopying, recording or otherwise) without the prior written permission of the author. Any person who does any unauthorised act in relation to this publication may be liable to criminal prosecution and civil claims for damages. Enquiries should be made through the publisher.

Cover design: Ultimate World Publishing
Layout and typesetting: Ultimate World Publishing
Editor: Jessica Whitehill

Ultimate World Publishing
Diamond Creek,
Victoria Australia 3089
www.writeabook.com.au

What people are saying about *Harmony for Couples ... A Divorce Lawyer's Ultimate Guide to Marriage Success.*

"What if you could find, marry and stay married to your guardian angel for life? After the wedding, honeymoon and 'pink cloud' phase has passed, how do you maintain the blush on the rose? Can you approach the forces at work in your marriage like those under the crust of the earth that crush, compress, stress, pulverize and meld, and in the end have a diamond rather than a broken collection? As a high-profile married man of 30 years, I found *Harmony for Couples* to be the perfect read for many seeking answers to these and many more relationship and marriage questions. Simply brilliant!"

Frank McKinney
Florida USA
6x Bestselling Author, frank-mckinney.com

"In these times when fewer people are getting married and are waiting much later to tie the knot, you'd expect the divorce rate to be minimal, but statistically it's comparatively high. I have great joy knowing that Joyce Khoo has written this book to help stop this momentum. She has drawn on her work experience with genuine life situations and provided practical advice and solutions that are more than theory. She describes the causes of marital breakdown and the consequential problems. This book is a must-read for anyone who is married or intending to marry to practise the principles for a happy and fulfilling life journey as a couple. Well done, Joyce! This book is right on time!"

Colin Cooper
Huddersfield United Kingdom
Chairman of Ministers Fellowship Global

"The contents of this book impressed me as being extremely good and spot on. I believe that this book will help a lot of people. Joyce has written in such a way that anyone can easily understand the principles and apply the lessons shared. I have been married for 42 years, have three grown-up children and three grandchildren. I have pastored my church for 35 years and personally counselled many couples. My wife and I have practised many of the lessons in this book, and we are still happy and in love after all these years. I highly recommend this book for couples to gain wisdom and values to build a strong and healthy relationship."

Agamemnon Sakellariou
Athens Greece
Senior Pastor of Hellenic Christian Church

"Joyce Khoo has a wealth of counsel to bring to couples by virtue of being a divorce lawyer as well as a pastor. There is a plethora of practical guidance for the conflicting maze of faith, beliefs, aspirations, hurts and legal alleyways that ends in divorce. I am sure you will read this with interest and gain new perspectives on divorce … and even lawyers!"

Bruce Laird
Melbourne Australia
Senior Pastor of Monbulk Christian Fellowship

"With one in three marriages ending in divorce today, there is a desperate need for help in making marriages better. This excellent book by Joyce Khoo is packed full of wisdom and insight for strengthening marriages everywhere. Drawn from years of experience and reflection, this book contains advice well worth listening to. I highly recommend it."

Mark Conner
Melbourne Australia
Speaker and Author

Testimonials

"After nearly 60 years of being happily married (with a few hiccups), I thought I knew everything there was to know about being in a committed relationship...I was wrong! This book is passionate, erudite, funny, and warm. There is a treasure trove of great advice based on Joyce's own experiences; 30 years of marriage to Kenny speaks loudly of authenticity, 20 years of legal work including family matters, and she has prepared couples for marriage. I highly recommend this truly amazing book for anyone contemplating marriage, and even for couples who have been married for a few decades, like me!"

John Gagliardi
Queensland Australia
Director at Haggai International Australia, Author

"As a therapist and healer of all issues including intimacy issues, many of my clients' problems are much more complex than just the physical. It's often a deep-seated issue within their relationship that prevents them from enjoying a fully satisfying physical relationship. The advice in this book is great. I love how Joyce keeps reminding readers to treat each other with the utmost respect, that everyone matters, which is so very important to a happy, satisfying long term connection. I believe that this book will help resolve couple issues in and out of the bedroom."

Anika Brizuela
Brisbane Australia
Therapist and Healer

"If you are contemplating marriage or looking for a way to keep your marriage on a solid foundation, then *Harmony for Couples* is the book for you. Joyce's vast experience as a lawyer and relationship counsellor has given her the opportunity to see firsthand what works and what doesn't work. Her book is full of practical advice that you will find useful whether you are single or married. Read it, embrace new ways, and get ready to reap the rewards."

Karina Ballesteros
Melbourne Australia
Director of Remar Australia

"This book is revolutionary for young couples! Joyce's coaching has transformed our lives and prepared us for marriage. We have experienced our relationship prosper from practising the principles in this book such as proper communication, how to resolve conflict, and boundaries. There are many gems of practical advice and real-life scenarios from her experience as a lawyer and from coaching couples. People of all ages, backgrounds and circumstances will greatly benefit from her insights into how relationships can work for the long term."

Sarah Lim & Jason Quah
Melbourne Australia
Conveyancer & Accountant

Testimonials

"Our love grew from a mutual love for ministry and music. Through her wise counsel and encouragement, we were married by her in Melbourne, Australia. We share many of the values that Joyce has included in this book, which we highly recommend as a must-read."

Joseph Lam & Ruth Foong
Singapore
Engineering Director & Worship Director

"We are so grateful to Joyce Khoo for her great insights and timely advice at every milestone during our courtship journey to prepare for marriage. The stories that Joyce uses in this book are personal, honest, and speak a great deal of truth. We have learnt valuable principles and practical ways to enrich our relationship."

Jee Tan & Shu Liew
Kuala Lumpur Malaysia
Business Consultant & Senior Manager

"This book will give couples practical guidance to achieve success in marriage. Joyce's coaching helped our understanding of what it means to be "one" and how to plant seeds now for the future harvest of true happiness in our family. Partnership and teamwork are keys. We recommend that you look out for the many precious jewels while reading this book."

Mary Wong & Denny Chan
Hong Kong & Macau
Accountant and Safety Manager

"I thank God for people like Joyce who understands the complexities of relationships. Under her care and guidance, she provides a dummy-proof blueprint to help couples succeed in marriage. I have learnt so much more about marriages from this book that will be a huge help for me in my search for Mrs Right!"

Shiva Raj Timsina
Bhutan
Evangelist

"In the world of #CoupleGoals and #RelationshipGoals we see couples falling for the idea of the perfect wedding and tending to build their marriage based on internet content. Our 'throw away' culture suggests that everything is disposable, even marriage. Pastor Joyce's book has helped us to look beneath the surface to where the foundation lies and has helped us to learn the practical steps how to nurture our marriage. You will be just as blessed as we have been in reading this book!"

Prashant & Srijana Pradhan
Banepa Nepal
Pastors of Ropheka

"A sensational collection of real-life stories and exceptional advice from an expert who has seen it all; the good, the bad and the ugly! This book will inspire every reader to have a successful marriage and give it the time, care and respect it deserves."

Toni Lontis
Gold Coast Australia
Author, Speaker, International Radio Host

Testimonials

"Marriage should be wonderful! It should be fun, exciting, passionate, full of joy, care, and support. It should hold you up when life gets tough. It should be healthy and positive. It breaks my heart that sadly, the reality is far from this ideal. Therefore, get educated, read this book, be open to change, and watch your life transform. I promise the principles in this book will greatly benefit both you and your partner."

Nicholas Green
Las Vegas USA
Camera Operator, Husband, Father

"In my opinion the market is flooded with information on how to throw the perfect wedding but severely lacks quality material on how to stay married! Make sure you keep this book on your shelf. This is a sensational reference tool for when things get tough, but also is an excellent refresher on how to keep the spark alive."

Eric Agyeman
Melbourne Australia
Founder of The Royal Hood

"Joyce has put her legal profession on the line and spilled the beans with her years of personal experience and professional eye to help you to avoid engaging a divorce lawyer and save on legal fees! This book contains highly practical tips and Q&A sections from people asking the same questions you may be asking. Joyce's wisdom benefits married couples as well as individuals going into relationships, and in fact, everyone in coupledom! "Don't go into love blind," she says. What does that mean and more? You've got to devour this book to find the answers."

Perryn Khoo
Melbourne Australia
Digital Marketer

"After 31 years of marriage, I discovered my ex-husband's infidelity and had no choice but to divorce him. I know firsthand the devastation of divorce on an individual, not to mention the financial ramifications, and I wouldn't wish it on my worst enemy! I love Joyce's book because she openly discusses many topics that I feel are avoided because of culture or religion. If your relationship has cracks, read this book NOW and follow the advice before it's too late. It's worth learning from others' mistakes and saving oneself from years of pain and regret!"

Maria Flores-Vivas
Nicaragua
Doctor

"A light-hearted and easy-to-read guide with practical examples. Joyce shares her tips and stories with her unique brand of humour. The stories are an eye-opener and bring clarity through our rose-tinted glasses during a time when we choose to believe only the best in the person that we fall in love with. A useful guide to have before and after marriage to keep your relationship fresh and fulfilling."

Linda Long
Melbourne Australia
Lawyer, Wife, Mother, Friend

To Kenny, you're sometimes impossible to live with, but mostly the best example of commitment, faithfulness, and friendship.

CONTENTS

Introduction	1
Chapter 1: Know What You Want	7
Chapter 2: It's Not All Beer and Skittles	25
Chapter 3: The Long Game	41
Chapter 4: He Said She Said	55
Chapter 5: Matters of the Heart	69
Chapter 6: Which Buttons to Push	85
Chapter 7: Taming Angry Hippos	99
Chapter 8: Under the Sheets	119
Chapter 9: Crafting Legacy	133
Chapter 10: Meet the Kinsmen	151
Chapter 11: Honeymoon Forever	167
Chapter 12: The Seasons of Love	181
Afterword	197
Works Cited	199
Acknowledgements	203
Speaker Bio	205
Notes	207

INTRODUCTION

As a young girl growing up in Singapore in the '70s, I swore never to marry. This decision wasn't born out of some hardened, feminist ideology, but simply that I didn't observe any happily married couples; my own parents included.

My dad ('Pa') grew up in a Buddhist family in Taiping Malaysia but relocated to Singapore to work as a police detective. He was adventurous, had a wide circle of friends, but was feared for his bad temper and unpredictable nature. Mum ('Mee') was the polar opposite of him. She was raised in a Christian family in Singapore, was well educated and calm, and fearsome as a school principal. They met through mutual friends and decided to create a life together. There were happy times when I was younger, but I recall my parents quarrelling a lot, and once, out of frustration, Pa asked me whether he should shoot Mee with his pistol.

When I was nine, we moved out from government subsidised accommodation on the outskirts of the city to our family apartment opposite the lagoon on the East Coast. With this move came a significant increase in financial pressure. Coupled with the stress of raising three children and their personality and culture clashes, my parent's marriage was wrought with friction.

By some miracle, my parents have remained married, and thankfully, Pa has mellowed with age. However, these experiences in my early, formative years did little to sell the idea to me that marriage was some type of Hollywood fairy tale.

This negative viewpoint was further modelled by other close family and friends, particularly my grandmother (Mee's mum), who apparently, dutifully looked after seven children while my grandfather partied up a storm with a rotating array of young women on his arm. Eventually, through a series of unfortunate events, or perhaps karma, he ended up a lonely old man and ended his life in the bedroom I later inherited … an ever-present reminder that marriage isn't all sunshine and roses.

There were many other woeful examples of marriage in my childhood, exacerbated by the archaic Singaporean Asian culture at the time where men were chauvinistic and had a superior complex, and usually the breadwinners. They were considered smarter than women, were always right, and had the final say. Most women were housewives, or if they did work, were paid much less.

By the time I was a teenager, I was happy to kill off the idea of finding my non-existent Prince Charming and decided to focus on more interesting endeavours. For a while, it worked.

I was somewhat of a 'Queen-Bee' in school – sporty, popular, and chased by many boys (and girls). After school hours were spent playing basketball, squash, cycling, and in the ocean windsurfing and canoeing. I loved hanging out with friends and caring for my menagerie of pets. My dedication to academics, however, wasn't quite so impressive and involved me cramming for exams, consuming energy drinks and offering up desperate prayers.

I made it to Singapore University but was more dedicated to sport, and in the first semester managed to win 22 gold medals

Introduction

for sporting events. I was one of the nation's top women squash players, and any leftover energy was channelled into scuba diving, preparing to be an aerobics instructress, and training for body-building competitions.

I certainly didn't need a man. I was a kick-ass semi-professional athlete, and an aspiring (per Mee's foresight) soon-to-be-lawyer.

Then, in 1989, I moved to Melbourne, Australia to pursue my studies, and here, I met Kenny, almost literally, the moment I stepped off the plane! He was 21 years old, came from a good Christian Malaysian family, was kind-hearted and serious. Unfortunately, he was not my type at all. He had a tubby physique and didn't share my sense of humour or passion for health and fitness one iota. Poor Kenny spent the next two years attempting to win my affection, and I kept him very much in the 'friend zone'. Then, through what I can only describe as a very spiritual set of circumstances (I won't bore you with the details), I was suddenly overwhelmed with the realisation that he 'was the one'.

Uh-oh.

In true metamorphosis style, Kenny smartened up his lifestyle, lost 20 kilos, and became my running, squash, and gym partner. Suddenly, 'Kenny the dork' became 'Kenny who makes me weak at the knees'.

By age 22, I was married to Kenny and have been ever since.

Despite the whirlwind match, it wasn't all smooth sailing. We fought a lot. We seemed to have different perspectives on just about everything; from how to cook char kway teow to how to handle our finances. However, one thing that we had in common was the lack of interest in having kids.

There must have been some divine plan at work because after completing my law degree, I spent two years at Bible College, and by some twist of fate, I ended up volunteering in Children's Church. Lord, help me! Give me locusts, a plague, angry Egyptian slave owners ... anything but children! Before long, I realised they weren't the snotty-nosed gremlins I had quite imagined. I began to see each child's unique personality; how curious they were, how beautiful and cheeky they could be.

One month after this course, I fell pregnant. Five years later, I fell pregnant again.

Thankfully, my misgivings about motherhood weren't all warranted, and I can say, hand on heart, that I thoroughly enjoyed raising my two sons, now aged 16 and 21. I've definitely learnt many valuable lessons from raising children, especially what not to do.

As much as my relationship with Kenny has taught me, it's my professional career that has truly educated me on what makes a successful marriage and what destroys.

I started out as a young, impressionable lawyer in 1996, then opened my own private practice in 2000 and named it Crossover Consultancy (now JK Lawyers). I also volunteered at a nearby Community Centre and charged a mere $30 per hour for legal advice where 90% of the cases involved family law matters. Back then, my views of divorce were rather fundamental, but I quickly got rid of the naïve and self-righteous attitude once I realised that the people before me were in such great distress, often numbed and in shock from the raw emotional upheaval of dividing their assets and breaking up their family.

In an ideal world, no marriage would ever break up. But they do.

Marriages break down all the time because people aren't perfect, and relationships are complex. It is with a clear conscience that I can say how honoured I am to be able to help my clients in what

Introduction

is often their darkest hour, and that I will continue to do so for the rest of my days. I've represented clients from all socio-economic backgrounds, nationalities, religions, ages and stages of life. Those with mental illnesses, health issues, sexual addictions, and criminal charges, as well as very down-to-earth, 'normal' clients whose marriage breakup stories aren't remarkable at all, but simply chalked down to "we don't love each other anymore."

After years of cleaning up broken hearts, I curiously found myself pursuing a parallel career as an ordained minister. But why? One would be bamboozled by such an oxy-moronic bi-vocational life.

Honestly, I guess I felt like I'd been in the family 'morgue' for so long, I wanted a chance to be in the birthing suite, to have a chance to nurture and educate families before the idea of divorce gestates. Through this second career, I've had the great pleasure of running pre-marriage counselling courses and officiating weddings, including that of my own brother and a few years later, my darling niece.

One day I'm helping clients divide their estate and organising visitation rights for their children, and the next day, I'm standing in a vineyard in the stunning Yarra Valley, pronouncing couples "husband and wife."

It's somewhat of a yo-yo set of credentials I've created and after more than two decades working in family law and a decade being a pastor and counselling numerous couples, I have observed similarities in the undercurrents leading to the breakdown in marriages.

It is with this collective wealth of experiences that I've written this book – because I really believe in marriage. The reality though, is that relationships require effort and investment to keep alive and vibrant.

Knowing how to maintain a healthy marriage isn't an innate skill that we're born with, especially if good role models weren't available in our formative years. School subjects don't tend to cover topics like "should you still have sex with your partner when they're being frustratingly impossible to live with?" Similarly, seeking marriage advice from friends, work colleagues, and the internet can be problematic.

I'm a firm believer in couples seeking counselling and professional help, but I do hope this book can be a tool to enhance your relationship, however that might look.

This book isn't just for couples whose marriages are on the rocks. It's for anyone who's unlucky in love, or those who have been in a previous relationship that may not have worked out. It's also for the romantics and the soon-to-be married, those in a committed relationship and those about to embark on a new one.

This book is for the heart-broken, those of you who've basically given up and are one fight away from dumping your partner's belongings out on the front lawn. For those of you brave souls who have suffered divorce and wonder if you'll ever find love and success again (spoiler alert – you can!)

Whatever state your love life is in, my hope is that you study the following pages. In them is what I consider the absolute essentials for ultimate success in your marriage and relationships. Obviously, I cannot begin to exhaust every dot and tittle topic relevant to marriage relationships, by the sheer fact that every couple will experience unique circumstances and exclusive issues.

Nevertheless, it is my intention that after reading this book, I never see you in my office, and maybe then I can retire from being a divorce lawyer and follow my other passion; becoming a world-class body-building champion.

One can dream...

CHAPTER 1

KNOW WHAT YOU WANT
~ WHAT TO LOOK FOR IN A RELATIONSHIP ~

"Marriage: 'Love is the reason. Lifelong friendship is the gift. Kindness is the cause. Til' death do us part is the length.'"
Fawn Weaver

Love is Blind

If the saying 'love is blind' has been the guiding mantra for couples, it is no wonder that so many marriages fall apart.

Some people go into a relationship with this belief or other well-intentioned advice. This causes them to:

1. Not worry about external appearances or how the life partner looks, because 'love' makes up for the lack of good looks, OR
2. Not look too much into the nature or character of the life partner, because 'love' will work everything out in the end.

This, 'no worries, she'll be right mate' attitude may work for some, but from my observation, this attitude has created shaky and weak foundations in many relationships.

I certainly would not want to go into a relationship with Jekyll and Hyde! Would you? Would you want to take the gamble that the person who courted you and showered you with loving acts and romantic words, and peppered you with gifts galore (Jekyll), turned out to be the extreme opposite (Hyde) after the wedding?

It is far more sensible to keep one's eyes wide open to see everything there is to see, to be fully aware of what to expect, and have a proper understanding and full acceptance of your partner before the wedding. Then after the wedding, have the liberty to close one or two eyes, so to speak, so as to overlook the other's shortcomings and faults, out of love and for the sake of the longevity of the relationship.

The Biggest Investment of Your Life

Let's be steely serious about this decision to be married to another person. It is the most wonderful experience one can have. From the discovery of chemistry to the desire to be with the person constantly, to the obsessive and infatuated thoughts of him or her. Love tingles can cause goose bumps all over, butterflies in the stomach, heart palpitations, sweaty palms, nervous energy, not to mention other bodily reactions – but more of that in Chapter 8 "Between the Sheets!"

When you feel this person is special to you and the one you wish to spend the rest of your life with, you really are giving up all of yourself over and expecting him/her to reciprocate by giving up all of himself/herself to you. Most significantly is the fact that you are investing your whole heart, life and resources into the relationship.

Surely, you would want to know what to look for in a relationship in your partner, and what to expect in the future.

Build a Mansion on a Good Foundation

There is no guarantee that life will blossom according to the great grand plan crafted at the outset, or whether life will throw curveballs at every chime of the clock. What's certain is this: to ensure that the exclusivity of the relationship between two people can stand the test of time, it must overcome every challenge, obstacle, trial, and finish strong. The couple must be mentally prepared to put in the necessary effort and resources into building the relationship, starting with the proper foundation. The hard work towards building connection and intimacy is not a once-off but must be continuous, regular, purposeful, and intentional.

Avoid Supporting the Statistic

I have heard it said numerous times:

> "Had I known he was such a person, I would not have married him, but I did not know, and that is why we are now in this mess."

> "Had I known this was how things were going to turn out, I would not have married her."

The aim is to work together with your partner through every issue of life that arises so that there is little room for regret. No one's perfect and this choice partner is a decision you made with good reason, so may I persuade you to work out the issues that have arisen and do what it takes to achieve perfection!

Choosing Mr Right and Mrs Perfect

There is no doubt that in choosing a life partner, the intention of both parties from the outset is, "for better or for worse" and,"'till death do us part". The key, obviously, is to make the best possible choice of the 'right' person, for the right relationship, for the happily ever after, forever.

Therefore, let's have a look at some of the golden rules and guiding principles in this exercise of choice.

Tip 1 – It is Not the Gold Rush

Take your time.

Even if your grandmother and aunties ask you the same question every time they meet you: "when are you going to get married?", and even if your mum and dad jump on the question: "is that your special friend?" every time they see you with a girl (or a boy), please remember that there is no rush to make a commitment to marry.

During one's younger years, it's often easier to meet potential partners through university, parties and part-time jobs. But as we get older and more serious about our careers, often these opportunities can diminish. If we don't make it a priority to carve out time to meet new people, we can quickly find ourselves middle-aged and single. Be open to meeting new people through various online, social, sporting, church, community, and professional groups.

Beyond looking out for suitable 'prospects' to start a relationship towards marriage, networking opens new horizons of awareness as there is so much to learn from other people's lives. But I counsel you to allow some time to pass, obviously not too long, to prove the partner of choice and have mutual opportunity to craft the values of your relationship together.

When my husband Kenny and I were young overseas students at Monash University, we were assigned Aussie 'parents' from our church, and they suggested, "six months maximum for one's courtship, and then marry; don't wait any longer." We became 'girlfriend-boyfriend' in June of 1991, and two weeks later we surprised our friends at a youth camp with the news of our engagement. Seven months later, we registered our marriage in Singapore. However, it is important for me to point out that for two whole years prior, we were working on building a friendship and dealing with issues that arose because of our differences that finally caused an ignition of the spark that swept us up in the whirlwind of courtship leading to marriage.

Tip 2 – Be Realistic and Reasonable

One may fall in love with his wife and expect her to be the homemaker. She, on the other hand, may expect to climb the corporate ladder striving for actualisation. Such a mismatch in expectations will probably lead to troublesome times. Will he allow her to be true to herself or insist that she sacrifice her ambition and become subservient to his wishes? Can there be a compromise? Or will it be better to end the relationship early due to the incompatibility of values?

The movie *As Good As It Gets* (Tristar Pictures 1997) portrays the principle that falling in love is accompanied by accepting all the quirky idiosyncrasies of the other person. Helen Hunt plays a single mother and waitress at a local Manhattan diner who is the only one who will serve Jack Nicholson, who plays a misanthropic obsessive-compulsive author who is rude and insulting to everyone. He comes to realise that his selfish offensiveness is ruining his life. His character softens and learns to love, firstly his neighbour's dog, then his neighbour, and then the waitress. She responds to his clumsy romantic efforts out of generosity and patience. And so, an unlikely relationship develops.

Much like this movie, the 'right' partner may not initially present as the ideal match, because realistically, true love is a process that is crafted by the couple through effort and time. Sometimes, your partner may be as good as it gets! Avoid building one's dream on fantasy because relationships are formed between two people with real flesh, real heart, real feelings, and memories. Make a conscious decision to cherish the life partner of your choice, and love them for who and what they are, warts and all.

Find someone down-to-earth, and even though your first impression of him may be 'boring', he may be the best partner for life who will treat you with respect and support to you to become the best version of yourself!

Tip 3 – Go for a Test Drive

Most people I know would not decide to purchase a car without first taking it for a test drive. Therefore, it makes sense for people to 'test drive' their relationship before deciding to commit to a permanent, lifelong marriage.

My recommendation is to allow a reasonable period of time, say 12 to 24 months, to learn about your partner, walk out life together, to create opportunities to observe his/her behaviour among mutual friends, share meals, experience social activities together like sports, playing games, and going out for some fun times. During these times, be watchful to observe his behaviour, his verbal and non-verbal expressions; learn about her interests and hobbies. Ask questions to understand his parents and siblings, his upbringing, the family's culture, and values. Discover her true colours through playful competition. Notice what prejudices or biases exist. Ask your friends for their opinions regarding your partner. I guarantee that this will be a huge learning curve into gaining insights about your prospective partner.

These are some things to look out for:

1. Character qualities such as honesty, respect for others, empathy, hard-working.
2. Values and philosophical belief system.
3. What's the attitude toward the opposite sex? Chauvinistic? Chivalrous? Rough? Gentle?
4. Any mental issues? Any fetishes?
5. What's the attitude towards children? Fear? Ignorance? Contemptuous? Excitement? A sense of wonder?
6. What's the relationship with parents like? Harmonious? Strained? How and why so?
7. Any dependency on substances (coffee, cigarettes, alcohol, drugs, chocolate)?
8. What about temper? Short? Even?
9. Any criminal record?
10. Any baggage from past relationships?

This list of 'due diligence' is not intended to be grounds for paranoia or extreme cautiousness. It is important to be aware of your partner's predisposition and expectations, as this can paint the picture of what the future may look like for your relationship.

I know of couples who were entangled in a web of problems due to a failure to do simple background checks. For example, I once advised a wife what her rights were because her blissfully happy marriage was suddenly disrupted when she returned home from shopping one day to find her husband trying to drown their baby in the bathtub. She was later informed by the police that he had a previous criminal record and had been known to be mentally unsound.

In another family matter, I represented a wife who wanted me to obtain court orders for sole custody of her two young children for her, because after ten years of marriage she discovered that her husband was a convicted paedophile.

Sandy, my client, appeared composed and sweet during her attendances at my office, and I was convinced from her instructions that her husband was the aggressor. The psychologist report painted her in a totally different light. She bullied and behaved hurtfully towards her family because she was unable to control her anger. Apparently, this couple's initial romance had clouded their ability to discern that she'd be the wife from hell and prevented them from seeking early intervention to preserve their marriage.

Therefore, I counsel you to find out as much as you can about your prospective partner, and yourself, as issues can be identified and worked on earlier before any commitment is made, and this is far better than the undesirable discovery afterwards.

I do recommend that couples undergo health checks with their medical practitioners to ensure all-round physical wellbeing. It makes sense for applicants of Australian visas to satisfy the public interest criteria by obtaining police clearance certificates. Similarly, it wouldn't hurt for couples to be open to mutually applying for police and working with children checks, according to the relevant guidelines in the state or country of residence. The information for these applications is usually readily available online through a simple search. The results may add spice to the many memorable experiences in a couple's journey towards marriage!

Tip 4 – Uncover Hidden Agendas

The biggest mismatch leading to a relationship breakdown can be uncovered and resolved early in the relationship by simply asking questions of each other and seeking to receive honest answers.

This story may be an extreme example, but I feel it's relevant here. It involves my client John, who was an accomplished businessman in his seventies, who had a voracious appetite for sex. John was pursuing marriage to his 'lucky lady', number three, whom he'd met through an online dating site. He asked me to assist with his sponsorship of the visa application for his fiance, while he travelled overseas to meet her and bring her to Australia. She was a successful businesswoman who'd remained single. I had a sixth sense she wanted the benefit of Australian residency status. After all, who would marry a seventy-year-old man of a different culture with whom you couldn't communicate due to a language barrier? Yes, he only spoke English, and she only spoke Mandarin! He assured me that the sex would be the glue for the relationship. Unfortunately, she left him almost immediately after receiving grant of her visa. Need I say that he was devastated?

I assisted Tamara with her sponsorship of her husband's visa application to remain in Australia. They presented beautifully on their wedding day. Her family supported them financially and set them up with a nice family home. He disappeared without a trace on the day he received grant of his visa. She was in shock and confusion when she contacted me. Sadly, she realised that the 'genuine love' was in fact only one-sided, and her husband had cruelly put up a clever pretence.

This type of preconceived hidden agenda is selfish to the core, extremely inconsiderate, and can cause great damage to the unsuspecting partner who, being genuinely in love, may have invested their best intentions and even finances into the relationship.

It is important for couples to each agree to the values upon which the relationship will grow as well as understand each other's expectations, needs and ambitions. The more the couple can agree upon, the stronger the ground on which the relationship will stand.

Find someone sincere, genuine, authentic, and who is mutually willing to build on good values.

Tip 5 – Understand Personality and Character Qualities

We are all wired differently, possess different personalities, are brought up in different cultures, and are endowed with different educational opportunities. We are groomed to future ambition (or lack of it) in different environments. Couples usually discover how opposite they are to each other, and it's important to work out the values and life philosophies early to minimise a rocky rodeo journey ahead. Imagine the analogy of two oxen put together to plough farming land. Both animals must carry the same yoke, head in the same direction, do the same work, and aim to achieve the same result. If both animals are not in agreement, if each animal pulls in different directions or have opposite work ethics, the animals will be at constant loggerheads, the yoke may eventually break, and their efforts (even while together) will fail to yield anything successful.

Therefore, learn about each other's personalities. Look out for good character qualities such as sincerity, honesty, respectfulness, patience, ability to listen, love, and humour. Look out also for show of pride, a contemptuous attitude, a critical spirit, and a tendency to complain. What similarities do you both share? What differences have you identified? Will he seek to force you to conform to his unilateral biased philosophy of life? Is she overbearing?

Many issues can be discussed and addressed earlier in the relationship while you are establishing your foundation for future years together. Even differences can enhance and strengthen a relationship, so long as you know how to work together and utilise the differences for mutual benefit.

Tip 6 – Equality and Roles

The most balanced relationship is one where mutual recognition of value and significance in the other exists, and from this equal footing, each assumes their respective role and fulfils their respective responsibiliites. I have witnessed countless relationships where, for example, the husband acts superior to the wife, and there is an imbalance concerning who controls the finances (while the other is powerless in the decisions as to how the family finances are kept or disbursed), how the children are parented, who has freedom of expression (while the other's voice or opinion is not worthy of being heard). Another example is where the wife does all the talking for herself and her husband.

Obviously, every relationship works differently, and perhaps your wife is a whizz at finances, and you barely made it past Year 8 Maths. Or maybe your husband is the next Jamie Oliver and loves to cook gourmet meals, whereas your idea of cooking is to throw a ready meal in the oven, let it burn and then order take-out at 10 p.m. We each have our own strengths and weaknesses and whilst we should always try and improve for our own self-development, sometimes it's worth calling 'time of death' on that thing you aren't any good at.

Let one's strengths cover the other's weaknesses. Avoid persisting in one's weaknesses and refusing to improve, adjust, and change, just because 'it's expected' or 'this is the way my parents/culture do it.' Know who you are and be secure in your uniqueness. Don't box yourself into a mould that is not a proper fit. If you've killed 57 pot-plants, it may be time to admit you don't have a green-finger. If your husband doesn't have a romantic bone in his body, rather than chastising him, consider taking over that department and be the official romance co-ordinator in your marriage – at least you're assured to have great dates! Roll with it.

I know one couple where the husband was brought up by an Italian mother who regularly cooked for crowds of friends and family without breaking a sweat while looking fabulously immaculate. Whereas his own wife found cooking for six people quite the stressful ordeal. After many fights and tears (on her account), they finally came up with a solution. Whenever they hosted a dinner party, the husband would either shop and cook himself, or order take-out meals for their guests. Suddenly, his wife became an amazing host as she was able to focus on what she was good at, preparing the house and doting on her guests throughout the evening. She also looked smoking hot as she wasn't slaving over a hot stove, which made the husband very proud. Now, they host dinners all the time. Win-win.

Thrive in your abilities. Remember, it's both of you against the problem.

Both parties must respect each other's unique personalities and seek to support and encourage the other to reach their best potential. Avoid trying to force your partner to become just like you, or to think like you do, or to do things your way. There ought to be an agreement as to the roles and responsibilities for how the home is run. Be supportive of each other's ambitions, gifts and talents. Encourage both partners to stretch and achieve their greatest abilities.

One of the advantages of marriage is TEAM! You want to be together, enjoy the synergy and reap the rewards of a great team effort. Good team members contribute and share equally.

With this understanding, each partner can assume the respective roles in the marriage that is best suited to him, whether it is the husband taking the lead in parenting, or the wife analysing which investments will yield the best returns for the future family needs. Do what works best for your marriage. Remember, it's YOUR marriage. If your friends judge you for not subscribing to traditional gender roles, it may be time to get some new friends who will love you both unconditionally.

When each is working to his or her strengths, the inevitable result is success, peace, and harmony in the relationship.

Find someone who respects you, puts equal value on you and treats you as a team player with equal say.

Tip 7 – Love

Love must be at the centre, the basis, and the cornerstone of every relationship. Love is the cherry on the mountain top of great experiences together.

What is love? Katharine Hepburn famously penned that *"love has nothing to do with what you are expecting to get, only with what you are expecting to give – which is everything."* (Hepburn 1996)

The definitions of love vary, but what seems absolute is the universal belief that love is one of the strongest and most powerful emotions of the human condition.

Love is about relationships. Firstly, you must have a loving relationship with yourself. Being whole within and without is a good starting point from which to be loving towards your partner. Love like that naturally culminates in the beautiful physical act of becoming one through lovemaking and intimate sexual activity. Find someone who is content in themselves, has a healthy self-image, who is secure and able to love others.

FAQ

Here are some of the Frequently Asked Questions that I have come across, together with my responses.

Genuine Query

"I've noticed that I'm attracted to the same type of personalities, and somehow these relationships do not last. How do I go about finding the right person for me without going through the same cycle of failure?"

My Advice

Let your focus in searching for a life partner be to discover as much as you can about the prospective partner. Date your prospects and be thorough with the 'interview' process, asking questions and being curious as to background, views on the issues of life, and who should take which roles in the marriage. Including your friends in social activities gives them the opportunity to observe and evaluate your prospect. Your friends no doubt will look out for your best interests. Obviously, take time to build a friendship, be objective and realistic, and certainly avoid being prejudiced or biased. Hopefully, from this place of knowledge and the wise counsel of your friends, you'll be able to decide who would be a suitable fit for you, and this next time around, the choice will lead to a relationship for success and not failure.

Genuine Claim

"We have great sex, and I am confident that a great sex life is the solution to all problems and challenges."

My Advice

The sexual experience is one of the most wonderful experiences one can ever have in life. However, arguments, quarrels and fights will sooner or later diminish or dissipate the pleasure in sexual activities. This is because human beings are not only sexual beings but also possess a soul that needs to be nurtured and fulfilled through meaningful connections. Sex may not be the solution for harmony in marriage. Instead, you may discover that it is the soul connections that enhance the sexual relationship.

Genuine Claim

"I think we look perfect together. All our friends acknowledge that we look like the perfect couple."

My Advice

There's nothing wrong with being proud that aesthetically you and your partner are a great match. In fact, it could be an indication that you have similar drivers, whether health, wealth or lifestyle. However, looks alone are not something to build a relationship on. Make sure this doesn't distract you from connecting to your partner on a deeper level, such as learning about each other's:

   a. Strengths, weaknesses, interests, character qualities.

   b. Ambitions, desires and dreams.

MY SUGGESTIONS FOR YOUR ACTION

1. How well do you know your partner? Make a list of what you know of the following, and then compare with your partner:

    a. Hobbies and interests

    b. Favourite food, sport, holiday destination

    c. Parents and siblings

    d. Likes and dislikes

    e. Strengths and weaknesses

    f. Dreams and passions.

2. Does your partner have the following qualities (or is willing to work towards possessing these qualities?)

    a. Willing to invest into building a friendship with you.

    b. Is down-to-earth and realistic about life, as opposed to being idealistic and superficial about the issues of life?

    c. Respects you as an equal, giving you the liberty to contribute equally in every aspect of your relationship?

3. Do you know what are your future plans? Write down your answers to the following, and then compare with your partner.

    a. Will both pursue work? Or one to be the homemaker?

    b. How many children to have?

    c. What education to give to the children?

    d. What type of pets?

    e. How much to save each month?

    f. Will you give to charity? Why not? What percentage?

    g. What investments do you wish to make?

ADDITIONAL RESOURCES

Try free online personality tests to learn about yourself and your partner, for example:
- https://discpersonalitytesting.com/free-disc-test
- https://www.16personalities.com

CHAPTER 2

IT'S NOT ALL BEER AND SKITTLES
~ THE REALITIES OF A RELATIONSHIP ~

"Love is not something we 'fall' into, but a complex art combining many skills and talents that take a lifetime to learn fully."
Sam Keen

Fantasy or Realism

Everybody wants a fairy tale ending to the story; the hero battles impossible challenges and achieves victory. He has saved the heroine, swept her off her feet and carried her off into the sunset, and they now live happily ever after. These movies and romantic stories are fictional and fantasy. They are idealistic and omit the mundane activities and routine issues of life's realities. One ought not to model one's marriage after fiction.

To make your marriage a success, it is vital to appreciate that wisdom, knowledge and understanding, as well as many other necessary ingredients, have to be gathered for building the framework and structure for a strong marriage. One cannot expect the relationship to succeed without any intentional effort, planning or strategy.

Cloud Nine

Falling in love ... the great sense of excitement ... nervous anticipation ... the mystery and intrigue. Will she respond to me positively? Will she reject me? What does he think of me? Will he love me?

When the love of your life says 'yes' to your advances and starts to respond with reciprocal love and affection, it is literally the most exhilarating time of one's life! The relief! The emotions, adrenalin, and pounding heartbeats. So much to discover about each other, so much of the world to explore together. Memorable dates and experiences over coffee, movies, walks in the parks, vineyard wine tastings, and weekend's stays.

The usual process could be as follows:

After the courtship period, the biggest key to success and longevity is simply taking hold of reality and figuring out what the basic needs are to make life together work! You must step out of cloud nine as quickly as possible and walk on level ground. Take off the rose-coloured glasses and start to plan married life with sincerity.

Road Map for the Long Journey

Every couple desires success and longevity. I say the journey is best commenced with a road map which has the end goal pegged, the direction clearly marked out, with pointers and checkpoints to keep you focused and on track. The journey is not a short sprint event to the finished line around the corner. Therefore, be mentally prepared for the long haul and expect long and straight boring roads, sharp curves and bends, sudden speed bumps to slow you down, pot holes to avoid, steep gradients upwards, and sometimes travels involving dark valleys and pain. In short, be ready for an adventure of all sorts of experiences, custom made for you.

The GOOD NEWS is that relationships can last forever, and I have had the privilege to interact with couples who have been together for thirty, forty, fifty years and longer. Below are some success tips that can hopefully help you. Perhaps YOU could be included in the Guinness World Records for the longest marriage!

Tip 1 – Healthy Self Love

The best preparation for marriage starts with YOU!

From my own experience, I remember somewhat hyperventilating at the thought of losing my independence and being joined to someone else for life. I could barely commit to a hairstyle, let alone a life partner. I spent a few months wrestling and in deep thought over whether to stay single or allow the process of friendship to lead into marriage.

Marriage will test the strength of one's inner self or expose what is hidden inside. I'm not saying that you have to be perfect, but it is beneficial for you to feel secure, be content, and not be uncomfortable being alone, before your partner arrives. Many people pursue a serious relationship hoping to solve the problems they are facing, when in fact, underlying matters left unresolved may sabotage and hinder any chance of a good relationship with someone else, such as the following:

- Healthy love for self.
- Mental soundness.
- Issues from past relationship(s).

Immaturity and relationships are not compatible, and the following tendencies will be counter-productive to a successful marriage:

a. Being overprotective of one's partner, and paranoia over his/her liberty to socialise and network, especially with the opposite sex.
b. Wanting control of every decision and activity.
c. Feelings of jealousy over his/her popularity.
d. Insecurity over the loyalty of one's partner due to low self-esteem.
e. Stalking your partner, checking the messages on his/her phone.

Therefore, prepare yourself well. Invest into nurturing yourself and developing a healthy and strong body and soul, because once married, it is far easier to look after someone else besides yourself from a place of wholeness rather than from a place of unpreparedness.

Tip 2 – Commitment

Marriage is a life-long commitment that begins on the first day and must continue every day afterwards until the time together comes to an end. Whatever the drama, distractions, seductions, and temptations, stay loyal to your marriage.

A good analogy is when someone becomes a disciple of say, the best kung fu master. He cannot dream or hope his master's kung fu ability onto himself or expect to possess the techniques by just reading the manuals. He must match his commitment to many hours and days of practical training and exertion of effort. He must repeatedly practice the techniques and moves until the physical responses become automatic and second nature. Marriage is similar. It involves hours of practising and mastering the relationship skills until the couple becomes well blended and the good marriage relationship blossoms.

Start with commitment at the helm, then add the unshakeable resolve to make it work. Keep this attitude and desire at the forefront of your quest for marriage success. Don't even consider failure or breakdown!

Tip 3 – Think 'We' more than 'Me'

Many people struggle to 'lose' oneself in the committed relationship because it feels extremely vulnerable and uncomfortable. Two persons 'becoming one' requires both to give up the 'I' that has dominated all of one's life and give way to the 'WE'. 'We' now must take precedence in everything. The relationship is no longer all about 'ME' and consideration must constantly be given to 'WE'. Instead of expecting what you can 'get' out of the relationship, expect to give to your partner and think of what you can invest into the relationship to make it succeed.

How do couples match up two different minds, two varying intellects, two education levels, two differences in upbringing and culture? How to blend differences in communication, perceptions, abilities, strengths, and weaknesses? If you are thinking, "Woah, how in guacamole will any relationship have any chance of success?" or "This sounds impossible!" But we are wired innately to desire companionship, friendship, and intimacy, and that compels us to look for 'the one'. The mystery and glory of relationship success arises out of balancing the assertion of one's boundaries, and the letting go of one's rights and preferences, so that 'we' or one's partner can shine instead of just me.

Tip 4 – Delay Sex

Lovemaking is a beautiful and exhilarating experience, and who can wait to get to this zenith of enjoyment? However, I advocate delaying sexual activities and sexual intercourse until a strong, life-long commitment has been made between the two. Why? Simply so that both parties can focus this early stage on building their friendship. This involves discovering each other's strengths, weaknesses, habits and lifestyles, and stress factors. It entails identifying areas in the relationship that need work to strengthen them. It also protects hearts from being broken if the relationship sours.

Once couples go down the path of French kissing, heavy petting, and physical exploration, the sexual appetite is awakened, and there is no turning back. While the intense physical pleasure is incredible, the sensation can give couples, especially those new to courtship, a temporary sense of 'happiness' or distract couples from the important foundational steps to take for the health of the relationship long term. Physical intimacy achieved does not mean that mutual understanding and emotional connection has been similarly achieved.

After getting married, continue to build the friendship while enjoying the romance, and observe how the connections made on the deeper, more meaningful level enriches the sexual union. What I'm about to say might sound old-fashioned, especially in this modern age, but sex was designed to be enjoyed within the sanctity of marriage. This is where my pastor's hat comes on but bear with me and read on. Before the invention of mainstream birth control, the idea of pre-marital sex (especially for women) was scandalous. Why? Because purity was considered a positive attribute. Saving oneself for one's husband or wife was a gift beyond any other. Of course, there were some other benefits; no sexual diseases or secret love children, but it was also because, at that time, religion played heavily into the culture. The Bible says that when two people have sexual relations, their spirits become one, and I believe this to be true. Albeit, women seem to form this emotional attachment much easier than men, there is a universal truth to this principle. The unity that sex brings is powerful, but without the cocoon of a loving, committed relationship, this type of unity is precarious. For all the freedom and good that birth control has given us, it's also done damage. There are no safety rails. Don't get me wrong, I'm glad the pill was invented, but while it may resolve the issue of unwanted babies, it has thrown a spanner in the works in that couples are now excused from firstly working on marriage principles and values that enable long term success.

I remember having a discussion with some colleagues one night over a glass of wine. One of the younger associates had just gotten married, and someone at the table cheekily asked, "How's your husband in bed?" to which she replied, "Fantastic! But I've never slept with anyone else, so I have nothing to measure him by. Probably for the best, because, at the moment, he's James frickin' Dean, and I like it that way." You've got to see the beauty in that statement. She thinks her husband is a great lover – and maybe he is – or maybe he's still got a bit to learn. Either way, she was delighted because she wasn't comparing him to a catalogue of past Casanovas. It's a far cry from the conversations I overhear in cafés when friends catch up after a one-night stand and critique a stranger's sexual prowess.

I encourage the exercise of self-control, practising delayed-gratification, and discovering the inner qualities of your partner, as these open the horizons of understanding and appreciating the love between partners that is deeper and more meaningful than just physical and sexual.

I once counselled Greg who, despite my advice and persuasions not to do so, divorced his wife (A) and abandoned his children to marry a work colleague (B) because she was a better sexual experience. Five years later, he approached A and asked if she would take him back! He was a well-educated and respectable man, holding a high managerial position and overseeing hundreds of employees. I suspect that he never put in the effort to get to know A properly nor developed a mature and strong friendship with her. This was probably the case with B as well. It seemed he pursued each relationship for the sexual experience and when the rubber hit the road, he wanted out.

Build your marriage on a good foundation, and then you can build a mansion of lovemaking that will last a lifetime.

My recommended process to build successful relationships:

Now because I'm a seasoned lawyer, it would be remiss of me to preach the 'wait till marriage' card without also acknowledging some of the pitfalls that couples can face when doing so.

Some couples wait until they're married to 'do the deed,' and believe because of their sacrifice and control, they will have the best sex of the lives. But this isn't always the case. I know couples who rush through the courtship stage to get married so they can finally have sex, but once the novelty of this wears off, are left realising that they didn't really love their partner, they were just, to put it bluntly, super horny.

Similarly, I know women who have remained virgins so long that they have completely shut off that sensual, sexual side of themselves. Then, when they marry, they have found adapting to their newfound role of 'sex kitten' very overwhelming. Suddenly, they are expected to get over the decades spent denying themselves and be a sex machine. I've heard this described as the 'angel complex,' meaning that they've been an angel all their lives and find it hard to shake off that role. Others have found sex extremely painful and their husbands who have 'waited' are rightly frustrated that their new wife is not able or wanting to engage in a sexual relationship the way they had imagined. These are by no means deal-breakers and can be worked through, especially with counselling or sex-therapy. But it should be noted there are cases where delaying sex till marriage has caused issues.

I know of one woman who thought she'd found the perfect man and they waited until they married to have sex. But it was only then that she found out her husband was a porn-obsessed maniac with an extreme sexual appetite, compulsive liar and cheat. After eight years of living like this, the poor woman filed for divorce. Now, if this couple had engaged in a sexual relationship before they were married, it could be argued she may have seen the alarm bells and saved herself years of abuse. However, I wonder if there were warning signs in the dating process that the wife possibly overlooked. This is why the friendship and courting stage should be thorough. Don't rush to the altar to marry.

On the flip side, an Asian couple I counselled were concerned when they hadn't fallen pregnant over a couple of years. When they sought professional medical help, they were shocked to learn that they hadn't actually had sexual intercourse! They thought just touching their genitals together would result in falling pregnant.

It seems inconceivable but remember, sexual education in many cultures can be vastly different. This shows the importance of communication, openness, and a willingness to get educated, to build a healthy sexual relationship. This isn't something to be embarrassed by.

Once you find 'the love of your life one', talk about sex. What works, what doesn't work. Get good at it! If there are issues between the sheets that can't be resolved, seek help from books and a sex therapist. Educate yourself on how to satisfy each other. I don't wish to burst any virgin bubbles here, but in reality, sex is a physical activity, and as such, many doctors and sex experts have produced material to explain how the body works for maximum enjoyment of this sexual activity. You just need to find the right education.

Tip 5 – Invest in Proper Education

Unfortunately, the one or two decades of education in our formative years is dreadfully remiss in teaching couples how to be successful in relationships and marriages.

In today's technological age, people mistakenly allow social media to be their source of education on relationships. One must be careful to test the opinions of people and discern whether they are wise, careless, or depraved. Social media tries to indoctrinate us into falsely believing that happiness is the right hair-cut, the coolest tattoo, the best abs or the strongest eyebrows. Furthermore, it gives the false ideology that true love is wearing matching outfits, elaborate romantic gestures, or being a travel blogging couple exploring the world. Whilst none of these things in themselves are bad, having social influencers teaching our youth is a dangerous source of education. These people are not experts; they are often paid by sponsors to portray a perfect life. It doesn't mean they have one or are qualified to give advice!

I was at an event where Dr Phil remarked while he was on stage that, "Instagram is like opening a can of dog food." He explained that people receive instantaneous feedback to their posts and may feel they are being examined and graded daily. If the comments are positive, people get an artificial high. If it is negative, they go straight down to an emotional low. People are not receiving proper validation, and cyber-bullying is occurring unchecked.

To build strong marriages, couples need to turn away from unrealities and seek out proper education to learn what is true love and what is false love. Faulty values lead to a weak foundation. Therefore, find good resources and even be guided by relationship coaches or professionals. This aspect of life is complex but can be incredibly rewarding. Just as you would expect a surgeon to have completed all the necessary qualifications and practical training before allowing him to diagnose your condition or operate on you, the same goes for marriage. Equip yourselves with the relevant knowledge and tools, acquire the necessary skills, then you can be confident to aim for decades of bliss together.

Tip 6 – Make Good Investments for Good ROI

Regular and proper investment into your relationship will yield a great return in the long run. Relationships can grow when couples spend quality time together, give special care and attention to actions that show love and build each other up. You cannot expect to be 'lazy' about your marriage and hope to enjoy amazing results. Therefore, put in the effort and make the sacrifices. Sometimes, you must shed tears and sweat before the breakthrough comes.

Spending meaningful times together and celebrating special occasions (birthdays, anniversaries) creates precious memories, each event being fitted to the whole marriage puzzle. Mark your diary to take daily walks and have weekly talks. Plan dates early and don't allow anything to cancel or postpone this time set aside for you both to enjoy together.

One of my clients, Barb, fell out of love with her husband because he was continually absent from family dinners, and she was tired of hearing his excuses and putting up with his passive-aggressive attitude. When we investigated into the matrimonial pool of assets, we uncovered a sizeable investment property portfolio worth millions of dollars! She was shocked at receiving our advice but pleasantly surprised. Unfortunately, it was his obsessive focus on creating wealth for the family's benefit that caused him to neglect his biggest investment of all – building meaningful relationships with his family.

Kenny and I are naturally task-oriented. We have both allowed routine activities to continue like clockwork and take precedence over building and investing into our relationship. Over the years, we have occasionally stopped to consider whether we were merely 'room-mates' or whether our relationship was of such significant value that special celebrational events were in order.

Kenny's preference and ideal date is at a crowded noisy café in Springvale over a 'cheap and good' delicious hawker style meal. Whereas I prefer to be refreshed while chilling out at a fancy restaurant over a fine dining meal with a full-bodied Shiraz casually chatting about the events in the week, especially after a long gruelling week of continuous hard work, meeting client requirements, and juggling my pastoral duties. One of the most satisfying experience for me was enjoying the Japanese edible craft of an ex-Iron Chef (now retired) who prepared an eleven-course degustation menu. I felt it was worth every dollar spent.

However, don't let money be the deciding factor of how you enjoy special times together. In the early days as a university student and later as new business owner, I assure you I wasn't doing much fine dining. Sitting in a car with your partner overlooking the ocean and eating take-away fish and chips can easily achieve the same result.

That being said, regularly set aside a small portion of your savings and reserve it for celebrations. There will be many reasons to celebrate, such as a promotion at work, a child's good report, the family football team's victory, even the capture of the neighbourhood fox that has terrorised the family's pet chooks. Celebrate the small and the big reasons to do so.

Tip 7 – Partnership and Team

Marriage involves partnership and teamwork. The rules of team sports are fair play, equal contribution, knowing your respective roles, and fulfilling your duties and responsibilities to achieve victory. It is necessary for team members to constantly communicate throughout the game to be on the same page, working towards the same objectives: score the goals, get to the finished line, ultimate victory of the team. Marriage is the same. Marriage partners must constantly communicate and check regularly that each has the same successes in mind.

In terms of leadership, no one partner can possibly fulfil every leadership role in the family. Therefore, husbands, arise to lead, but allow your wife to lead in her areas of strength too. You are a team, and you will complement each other by the different roles you assume since you both will have unique strengths and abilities. Wives, you must take up leadership in areas that you are naturally gifted and passionate about, so don't abdicate your rightful place. Together, the synergy can make your marriage exponentially stronger!

As equal partners, have mutual respect, share the authority, work together to accomplish the goals for the family while co-sharing the burden. Two are better than one.

I acted for Zina, who was devastated that her husband had one day returned home and without notice, packed his belongings into his car and drove off without turning back. Their three children were none the wiser. Through the court process, I observed that he had tried to be the best husband and father, but had become overwhelmed with bearing the burden of being 'the man of the house,' the sole income earner (from two jobs), and the manager of all the household finances and paperwork. He'd had the last straw and thrown in the towel. My client had assumed a subservient role out of her cultural indoctrination, and this had caused the scales of responsibilities to become imbalanced. Interestingly, she had been a high-flying corporate accountant before the marriage. What a shame for her to have buried her abilities and avoided putting her hand to the plough and taking a bigger role beside her husband, which she was obviously capable of doing.

Genuine Claim

"We're the same as other couples. We put on a happy front, but behind closed doors, it's not pretty. That's just marriage."

My Advice

Marriage is not a burden to bear. Overall, it should be a positive, happy experience. Healthy marriages thrive, and yours can too! If you feel your relationship is rocky, get counsel from a mature couple whom you trust, seek the help of a relationship coach or a counsellor. Put in the effort to work through this season without delay. The temperament of your marriage is truly in your hands to control.

Genuine Claim

"My partner is traditional. He won't change his ways."

My Advice

A common problem in marriages is the clash of culture and values. There's no easy fix. However, you could try the following approach:

1. Voice your issues calmly.
2. Ask questions to understand his mindset.
3. Find a compromise.
4. Be patient and encourage mutual personal growth.
5. Align yourself with other couples who may have faced similar issues for support and empathy.

Genuine Query

"We married because we were set up by our families. How do we bring 'love' into the equation?"

My Advice

Take a down-to-earth approach. This can help any relationship gradually transform into a loving, beautiful one. Consider what positive attributes you each appreciate of the other. Plan family projects together, celebrate the completion of each. Invest into building your future together. Appreciate your individualities and uniqueness. Praise, compliment and encourage one another. Celebrate strengths, cover weaknesses, and love will follow!

> **MY SUGGESTIONS FOR YOUR ACTION**
>
> Through my work with couples, I've noticed these factors recurring as stress points. Have a go at mutually discussing these points to better understand and support each other.
>
> - Feeling overweight.
> - Not enough exercise.
> - Not enough time ... to sleep ... for self ... for family and friends.
> - Too much work.
> - Not enough money.

Additional Resources

Read *Men are from Mars, Women are from Venus* by John Gray (Gray 1992).

CHAPTER 3

THE LONG GAME
~ SETTING GOALS ~

"When we recognize that we don't have all the time in the world, we see our priorities most clearly."
Laura Carstensen

When Kenny and I were newly married, we were young and short-sighted. Our goals were short term and focused on doing what was necessary to meet the basic survival needs of the family including securing financial stability, accumulating material possessions, and setting aside reserves for entertainment and short holidays. I believe if we had better vision then, our goals would have helped us work smarter, I would have done many things differently, we would have raised our children better, and I definitely would have pursued a more balanced life. Thank goodness we grew wiser with the passing of years, and these days, we are more disciplined and regularly sit down to discuss long-term goals to steer the marriage and family in better direction.

Setting Goals is a Healthy Exercise

During my work as a marriage celebrant, I've seen my fair share of wedding dramas. From future in-laws negotiating over the dowry, to which niece and nephew gets to be the flower girl and page boy, and even one couple having to conduct their wedding ceremony in an empty church building while streaming live for their guests to witness the event electronically.

For most couples, the wedding is the first major goal to start off the marriage relationship. The planning period seems to be the initiation rites to marriage, the litmus test to show how strong or weak is the couple's communication, conflict resolution, compromise, leadership, and delegation. Deadlines and stress with making decisions over big and minute details such as venue, decorations, clothing, colour theme, gifts register, photography, video, and putting on the show during dinner. It's all for this one goal: get to the altar, say "I do", and then party! Is this a good goal? Yes … if it ends well!

I know a few couples who had the most magical wedding experience but broke up within the year afterwards. One divorce matter I previously worked on involved preparing the paperwork for dividing the wedding presents between each partner.

Goals provide direction, give purpose, and help you identify distractions. When couples can see the destination, they can align values, clarify focus, and deal with issues that arise along the way efficiently. Challenges along the journey will test the strength of the relationship, whether it will buckle and falter, or whether the couple will do what is necessary together to achieve a breakthrough.

To have a 'great' marriage, couples must firstly define what is 'great' to them, and then set goals for each aspect of their lives together. Without goals, a marriage can track along vaguely and ambiguously through life. I've seen numerous relationships take off on a high note of romance and emotions, and then over time, become stuck in an impasse. One of my clients is a perfect example of this. Before migrating to Australia, she was a successful lawyer, and her husband was an accountant. They had a short but passionate courtship and a destination wedding in the Bahamas. Whilst breathtaking and decadent, there were disagreements at every level. It turned out he didn't want a big wedding or the price-tag to match, but the wife fancied herself as somewhat higher up the social ladder than they really were. Their goals were not aligned. Upon their arrival in Australia, and up to their eyeballs in debt, they led completely separate lives. She chased after the glitzy lifestyle, VIP clubs, yachting, making friends with celebrities, while the husband spent his time focused on creating a sustainable life and being a present father to their two children.

Another client had a similar experience. He was a hard-worker, good looking young man, and had made a small fortune in commercial real estate. During his youth, he'd kept his head down and saved, saved, saved. He owned a three-storey house in one of Melbourne's most elite suburbs, had the sport cars, the career … he just needed the girl. And sure enough, she showed up. She was in between jobs, had a couple of kids from a previous marriage and was $200K in debt. But she was stunning and charismatic, and quickly won him over. After a hot and heavy courtship, they were engaged and highly active on social media. She moved into his house, the wedding invites were sent out, and that's when it all came unravelled. She had a mean, violent streak. She'd throw knives, vases, and would threaten him physically and emotionally. By the time he ended up in my office, he was a mess and suffering PTSD. All he wanted was a wife to share his incredible life with, and all she wanted was an easy ride and a good-looking man to take selfies with.

Make sure your goals are aligned and not superficial. If your goal is to work hard, save and have a family, best not to shack up with someone that has no outward showings of those attributes. Debt, laziness and anger are not 'wife material' even if she does look great in a bikini.

Have Vision

It may require some time and effort for the couple to work out their vision for the future of their marriage and family, but it's not difficult and is certainly a positive step forward. Once you dig deep, ask questions of each other, and consider what you want your relationship to look like in the future, it will be easy to set goals.

Goals Evolve

Young couples in their early 20s could have simple goals such as, "I want a happy marriage." This is perfectly all right because this 'simple' goal will compel the couple to do whatever it takes and make whatever adjustments necessary to ensure that the marriage is 'happy,' including how you speak to each other, curbing the sharp tongue and keeping passion under control because passion expressed can appear angry when that may not be the intention at all.

Couples in their mid-30s could have goals to start a family and fund the expenses associated with one, two, three or more children. This might mean moving out of an apartment and into a large family home.

Couples about to retire may have goals to travel to exotic countries overseas or go caravanning around Australia.

Goals vary and evolve through the different stages of life as both partners grow and mature.

Surface Goals Are Hollow

Some couples fall into the trap of basing their goals on shallow ideals such as how perfectly they look as a couple. They seek to become the envy of everyone else by being the best looking, most glamourous couple in town. This problem has become more prevalent with the rise in popularity of social media and can be seen with hashtags like #couplegoals. It's no longer enough to be a happy couple; now there's pressure to be a gorgeous couple with the perfect house, glamorous holidays, expensive dates, and pets.

I would recommend to 'forget' this goal and to 'get real!' If you are being influenced by keeping up with the Joneses, Hollywood movies or social media, re-evaluate your measure of success. As appealing as many Hollywood couples' lives appear, these commonly crash and burn, ending in embarrassing cheating scandals and quickie divorces. Eating at the best vegan restaurants, attending VIP events and having 5-star holidays are all well and good, but if that's the foundation your relationship is built on, it's bound to fail. Be honest, if your partner is obsessed with this type of relationship, do you really trust her to be there for you when times are tough and when the cameras aren't on? Is he a fair-weather mate, or a forever mate?

Some girls go into a relationship just to 'have fun'. Some guys are merely 'trying out' to discover what a relationship is like. Neither of these reasons makes for harmonious, long-term relationships. As pleasurable as relationships should be, make no mistake, they are work and require self-sacrifice. It is only a matter of time before bills, babies and big decisions occupy a significant part of the couple's life. It is wise for any couple to be prepared and sufficiently equipped to handle the responsibilities, pressures and issues that accompany relationships. Goal setting and planning are the first steps in this preparation.

Matt told me he wanted a wife to love and serve him, make babies and tend the home. This could stem from culture or family background, selfishness or insecurity. I have seen husbands wanting their wives to wait on them, be at their beck and call, and treat them like royalty. I have also seen wives wanting the husbands to focus their whole attention on them, pander to their every need, and pamper them with love and physical touches.

May I let you in on a secret? No one person can fully satisfy the needs of the other. This is not humanly possible. It would require someone with supernormal ability, and I'm confident you know it's not your partner! It would be exhausting for the 'love-slave' in the marriage to constantly try to please the other. It is also detrimental when the other's expectations are not gratified. I have unsuccessfully counselled a few people who had lost interest in their partner, become resentful and refused to try again, because of their partner's self-centred disposition.

Ironically, our personal fulfilment comes from practising healthy self-love, selfless love in action, mutual giving out, serving the other, cherishing and nurturing each other, while simultaneously building the home and pursuing life's goals together on an equal footing.

Have a good, honest look at your goals and test your core desires to see if they are fluffy, airy-fairy, superficial or unrealistic. Be humble, forsake your pride. With harmony and longevity in mind, agree together to work towards setting better goals.

Go Deep

When couples convert from perceived success to what comprises true success, partners can begin to focus on fundamental issues as listed below.

a. Internally, develop these values that support harmonious relationships: honesty, respect, thankfulness, hard work and a spirit of excellence.

b. Relationally, agree to resolve past issues, deal with conduct ingrained from upbringings or previous negative experiences, overcome dysfunctional behaviours, and spend time to connect with, understand, nurture and support each other.

c. Externally, partners can decide what is exemplary behaviour. Show the children love and enable them to feel secure. Be faithful and loyal to each other, be diligent in earning income and spend wisely. At the same time, maintain good social and community connections with family and friends.

Couples ought to also work together to achieve clarity in these areas below.

a. Roles – Who will be the homemaker? Who will do which household chores?

b. Career – Who will earn the income? Pursue employment or business?

c. Income – What is the budget? How much income is needed to cover all the expenses? Are the expenses necessary or indulgent?

d. Savings, investments, insurances – How much should be set aside for emergency needs? What costs are involved to visit family living overseas? Should a children's education fund be established? What types of investments should be purchased? Should we take out insurances for life, total and permanent disability?

e. Children – How many? What are our parenting styles?

f. Social – How much time can I spend with my friends without my partner? Can I pursue my hobby? Should we limit the time spent on social media?

I agree that goal setting at this level is extremely unromantic. There are a myriad of areas in the relationship to which goal setting can focus. This can be done in a business-like fashion or in a more relaxed environment, even enjoying the process of planning, brainstorming and making decisions together! Create a conducive ambience filled with candles, a glass of wine, a chill-beat playlist on Spotify, while working with paper or a laptop. Set aside time and space for this. Preferably avoid setting goals when you know of obvious distractions such as the footy finals game on TV, feeding the baby, or when the in-laws are visiting.

Surprisingly, goal setting may lead to identifying limiting beliefs within oneself that require attention, such as:

- I lack motivation.
- I fear the unknown.
- I do not believe this is achievable.
- I can't change my partner's outlook on life.
- He's so stubborn.
- She's such a scatterbrain.

A marriage is strengthened when the inner moral fabric of both partners is strong. This includes commitment, faithfulness, perseverance, mutual encouragement, taking responsibility, owning the goals, and being accountable to show positive results. All these qualities will enable the couple to go above and beyond what they set out to achieve in life together. Through the process, they can experience healing, growth, more chemistry, and greater love.

Perhaps make one of your primary goals to bring out the best in your partner and mitigate and bolster your partner's shortcomings with your strengths!

Career & Marriage

Couples must also address goal setting for weightier matters such as finances and sufficiency, and the need to support one's partner fulfilment and actualisation. These are obviously necessary and help to enhance romance. Be realistic and start discussing these essentials early and at regular intervals during the relationship.

Whatever roles each partner assumes, they both must learn to understand the responsibilities, appreciate the effort, be aware of stress factors that accompany the respective roles. For example, the career husband must learn the value of showing appreciation to the homemaker wife, acknowledging her struggles when managing the home and the children 24/7. It is important to voice to your partner, for example, "Darling, you are such a patient and loving mum. I can see you're struggling with Bob's tantrums. How can I help?" The homemaker wife must not take for granted the career husband who endures many consultations with challenging clients, dealing with internal politics at the office and dodging crazy drivers on the road. The wife should acknowledge and voice her appreciation and encouragement by saying something like, "Honey, I'm so glad you are home. You're such a hard worker. I hope that the company knows how lucky they are to have you. Tell me about your day."

Both partners must give each other space to wind down, while making 'couple time' a sacred goal. Usually, both are exhausted at the end of the day, so best not to do goal setting and make long term plans when energy levels are low. Save the nights for low-level conversations. If tensions and fatigue cause sparks to fly, try to deal with anger before going to bed. Going to bed angry is a no-no. It's especially exacerbated if one simply drops off to sleep straight away, while the other suffers insomnia from feeling unjustly treated. Waking up with unresolved anger is the worst way to start the new day.

Boundaries

Boundaries help to keep you whole and safe. It is important to know and understand 'me', mark out your personal space, and decide what you will or will not allow to come inside your personal space.

Many couples do not know how to practice setting and keeping boundaries, which is important in many different relationships, even in marriage! If you let everything touch and affect you, it is no wonder that your life is an unending emotional roller coaster ride and you feel like a reed blown about by the wind. Because of this, many give up on their marriages.

The authors of *Boundaries in Marriage* (Cloud & Townsend 2003) describe four types of boundaries:

1. Physical boundaries – what can and cannot touch me.
2. Mental boundaries – what thoughts and opinions will I allow to make an impact on me.
3. Emotional boundaries – getting in touch with my emotional self, separating myself from negative, harmful, manipulative emotions of others.

4. Spiritual boundaries – what is right and wrong, my alignment to the godly values and convictions formed from my spiritual beliefs.

Having healthy boundaries in place will enable the couple to recognise occasions of misbehaviour and thoughts that must be adjusted. For example, the husband is over-protective or too controlling, or if the wife lacks trust or has unfounded suspicion. They both need to discuss what is healthy caution and what paranoia must be discarded. Then perhaps decide as follows:

a. I will not stay outside with my office mates after 8pm on Friday. I value investing into building our marriage, and therefore, I will return home by 8:30pm to spend time with you.

b. For my many meetings with clients, I will ensure the only physical contact I have is a handshake. You do not have to fear that I will entertain others' flirtatious ways because I will stay faithful and loyal to you only.

With effective boundaries, the couple will comfortably welcome the addition of children into the marriage relationship circle and handle the needs of the children in a good balance of boundaries and priorities amongst all the other aspects of family life.

Genuine Query

"I am not good at making or keeping goals, so how do I start?"

My Advice

Setting goals takes effort, time and focus. It is best done together with your partner rather than alone. The encouragement and opportunity to brainstorm can help to clarify and solidify the details of the goals. Start by deeply considering what you would like to achieve, for example, a happy marriage. Well, what does that look like? What does your partner look like? What do you want to look like? Additionally, invite a trusted friend or someone who can walk you through this process. An independent, trusted person can ensure goals are realistic and you are held accountable to achieve what you decide to accomplish.

Genuine Claim

"I have set many goals and am good at starting. Unfortunately, I never seem to finish what I started or achieve any."

My Advice

Once you have a goal, work backwards and break it down into smaller goals to accomplish over specific times (daily, weekly, monthly, yearly). Start with completing one goal, then add another goal, and keep going till you get the hang of it. Find someone to keep you accountable.

For example, write down one goal for each day that **you** can aim towards.

Day 1 – Go shopping for shoes (to achieve new year's goal to walk 10,000 steps daily).

Day 2 – Walk 30 minutes during lunch hour.

Day 3 – Sleep before 12am (to stop burning the midnight oil).

Day 4 – Compliment my partner during dinner.

Day 5 – Spend 15 minutes with each child before they sleep (building relationships).

Genuine Claim

"There is too much going on in my life already. I cannot add any more to my life, let alone new goals."

My Advice

Goal setting is not an addition to your current load. It can simply be a tool to clarify the current vision. For example, to have space at fifty to contribute to charity work, your goal could be to rearrange your routine life to free up time for this pursuit, by say working four days instead of five. Therefore, if you want to spend time with your partner, you'll need to restructure your schedule to fit in meaningful activities with your partner. If your marriage is a priority, goal setting will be a necessity, and you'll readjust everything else around this priority.

MY SUGGESTIONS FOR YOUR ACTION

Do you have a vision for your marriage? Do you have a five or ten year goal? Write down all the details then discuss with your partner.

1. Consider what you'd like to achieve in the next six months (conceive a baby, renovate the kitchen, read a book on communication, sleep more each night).

2. Notice what you both disagree over. Notice the differences in thoughts and opinions. Ask questions to understand each other better.

Additional Resources

Read *Boundaries in Marriage* by Dr Henry Cloud and John Townsend (Cloud & Townsend 2003).

CHAPTER 4

HE SAID SHE SAID
~ THE ART OF COMMUNICATION ~

"Ultimately the bond of all companionship, whether in marriage or in friendship, is conversation."
Oscar Wilde

Communication is a huge factor causing relationship breakdown. Somehow, despite all the investment of time and resources into receiving the best education, couples generally fail at effective and successful communication. An American divorce lawyer observed that his clients often claimed the reasons for their divorce was due to money, sex, or growing apart. He felt that in almost every case, these complaints were in fact symptoms of the real cause: a lack of regular communication. He said this: "If couples would make a point of setting aside time to talk about what is going on with each of them and to communicate their real feelings, I think that far fewer of them would end up in a divorce lawyer's office." (Silberberg 2016)

Basic Human Nature

Communication is a way of life that starts from before birth and doesn't cease until one takes his or her very last breath.

Babies give out cues to tell parents, "I'm hungry," "I want to play," or "I want to sleep," and parents must discern babies' cries and body movements for a happy relationship to exist.

As we become teenagers, we learn to communicate with parents, teachers, and friends to juggle the logistics of school, part-time jobs, social, and family obligations. The same is needed within a marriage. Frequently interaction is key to stay on top of household requirements, children's activities, and to keep informed of each other's career.

How Communications Break Down

Some couple relationships are estranged with little or no audible communication. The home atmosphere is tense and oozes hostility from the mutual cold shoulder and silent treatment of each other. Other couples are interacting all the time but may be abusive or aggressive, and this is not healthy nor edifying. From my observation, where poor communication persists, the risk of marriage breakdown will be high.

Couple Communication

Couple communication nurtures friendship and solidifies the marriage and can progress from the superficial into the deeper, more meaningful level of the heart and soul. With regular practice, couples will gradually overcome any insecurity and fears and become comfortable with transparency and vulnerability in sharing one's deepest darkest secrets. When couples feel sufficiently safe to share their innermost secrets, they will reap bountiful rewards because this type of connection and intimacy in the marriage is pretty darn special.

I sincerely believe that successful couple communication is the key to resolving issues such as anger, secrecy, alleged incompatibility, trust, withdrawal, arguments, even infidelity.

The following communication styles are unhelpful and can weaken couple relationships.

Censored

It is vital to understand that, for true happiness and success, each party must have equal ability and liberty to voice feelings, opinions, and make decisions. Some cultures propagate unequal power and authority in marriage, and different levels of freedom in one's expression. A dominant husband may be a bully such that he exercises full liberty to speak as he wishes but limits his wife and prevents her from voicing her opinions and feelings freely. An overbearing wife may hen-peck the husband and nit-pick everything he says. She may 'shoosh' him into silence because she sincerely believes he cannot possibly have anything to share that is worth hearing or considering.

In marriage, censorship of expression is not healthy. Both partners must have the ability to speak, express oneself, and banter without fear of being silenced. There must be freedom to ask questions, seek clarification, be heard without feeling judged or criticized.

Pretence

Some couples shove their issues under the carpet for a quick resolution. Just like the proverbial ostrich that sticks its head into the sand when trouble appears because it believes that since the issue is out of sight, it's therefore non-existent.

Conflict often surfaces when a major decision is required, and either one or both partners refuse to confront and deal with it, or deal with the issue wrongly. The avoidance could be due to immaturity, a lack of knowledge, refusal to understand, procrastination, fatigue, unfounded fear, or a host of other reasons.

The bottom line remains that turning a blind eye to an obvious quandary and pretending the issue does not exist does not lead to the problem evaporating into thin air. The problem remains. The couple may put on a façade and act 'normal' but beneath the charade is a live volcano with lava building up amidst bubbles of denial, excuses, blame, hypocrisy, insincerity, resentment, or bitterness. This lava is waiting for the opportune time to erupt without warning.

Distractions

The 'too busy' phrase is a cliché and a cheap shot at making excuses for not communicating. If the couple cannot graduate past 'functional communication' into true 'couple connection,' this avoidance will sabotage the longevity of the marriage. I agree that life can be extremely busy pursuing careers, furthering studies, engaging in sport, exercise, and enjoying social activities. You might be doing charity work or community services, which is commendable and magnanimous. And yes, the home, children, garden, and extended family all make justifiable demands on one's time. However, these distractions appear 'urgent' and probably shout the loudest to get your attention. In truth, they rob your marriage of what is important and necessary: quality time spent together communicating in a deep and meaningful heart-to-heart way that nurtures and strengthens the marriage.

Couples can spend six hours on a Sunday binge-watching their favourite TV show on Netflix, but neglect to spend six minutes with each other understanding the other's mindset and feelings, working out a way to live in harmony in spite of their unique characteristics and idiosyncrasies.

Red Bull

The 'red bull' type of communication occurs when one feels he must bulldoze his way through because she is not listening or understanding. It's a bullfight filled with aggressiveness. Such behaviour could be due to stress and tension built up from work. It could also be that she has not confronted her fears but lashes out in self-defence and self-protection. The unspoken rule of this attitude is that victory belongs to the 'loudest.' This bully mentality is accompanied by tantrum throwing, threats to get 'my way,' intimidation, manipulation, and force. Physical force, derogatory comments, and denigrating your partner in front of others are negative examples. The worst outcome is for the heat of the moment to lead to regrettable consequences.

There is a place for some level of intensity and sometimes high-volume expression, which may be healthy to relieve bottled up negative emotions. However, the conclusion is not always positive or edifying. It often leads to greatly exaggerated fights over a tiny, insignificant issue. It is necessary for both parties to promise to remain calm, rational, and patient while listening to the other. Firstly, to gain understanding. Secondly, to work out a way that satisfies the tolerance level of both parties and one that's mutually acceptable.

For years, Mort constantly shouted at his wife, threatening to quit the family business, and was bombastic about his feeling victimised by her decisions to purchase Chinese medicine from overseas. He feared the risk of a customer's death from mis-prescription and the ensuing lawsuit would cause the loss of the family's savings. After many heated arguments, Fanny consulted a relationship coach and learnt to make Mort promise to behave in a mature and professional manner. She explained that she understood his low tolerance for risk and high need for self-preservation. She then established a new company without his involvement to continue taking import of the Chinese medicine for profit. This solution was acceptable to him. Finally, the couple found peace.

Hidden Meanings

Couples may practice nonverbal communication, for example, the use of body language through the silent or cold shoulder treatment. Often this sort of communication is indirect and devious. The real message is 'hidden,' and the other partner is left to guess and work out what the silence is really trying to communicate. If you notice your partner giving you a passive-aggressive attitude or being stubborn or dismissive, then there's probably deep-seated offence(s) at the root. There may even be feelings of resentment and hatred. This subtle or covert form of expressing oneself is highly selfish and self-centred. It may be intended to punish and is unfair and unreasonable towards the other partner because one is intentionally not communicating with honesty.

John sought my help to divorce his wife only after three years of marriage. His wife wanted to have her mother and siblings live with them. He wanted intimacy with his wife and newborn baby without the other three relations in the house. Neither of them said anything. He became withdrawn emotionally. She was distracted with the baby and didn't read his cues. One day he just walked out of the marriage and never returned.

What is Couple Connection?

This type of communication enables a couple to:

- Connect – while maintaining individuality, two hearts uniting as one.
- Relate – there is rapport and empathy because two minds have a mutual understanding.
- Engage – where two wills become involved in each other's plans and intentions.

My philosophy of such communication is this:

1. Two parties achieve peace when there is understanding; otherwise, there is tension, offence, and bitterness.
2. To attain understanding, both must 'give' explanations, or be 'willing to receive' information. Unwillingness to give or refusal to receive will prevent understanding.

By exchanging information through speaking, writing, or some other medium, the relationship is deepened, widened, and heightened, leading to greater intimacy. After all, couples that commit to a long-term relationship intend to share their lives together, to walk in partnership, to climb all the mountains and scale the valleys, hand in hand. You now possess the key!

Communication takes time. Couples must mark their calendar and devote to investing into their marriage in a way that is best suited to their lifestyle. For example, suggested times together could be as follows:

- Daily for 15 minutes after dinner, discuss the day's events and the plans for the following day(s).
- Monthly date.
- Yearly night away from the family.

When together, your communication may consist of superficial chit-chat, addressing issues, confronting problems, planning the future, sharing personal feelings, desires and ambitions, dreams and hopes. Anything really. Whatever fuels the love, creates greater appreciation, draws you closer to each other.

Here are some guidelines and pointers to support your communication adventure, which I encourage ought to be internalized and practiced as often as possible.

Tip 1 – Verbal Communication

This is of paramount importance in a relationship. Today, verbal communication can occur without being physically in front of the other person. Couples can chat via video call, FaceTime, Zoom, GoogleDuo, which is great for long-distance relationships, and makes my university days feel ancient and me feel like a dinosaur. Because of technology, there's really no excuse not to find twenty seconds every day to send a cute message to your partner. These little tokens of affection tell your partner that s/he is still important no matter how busy you may be.

Be mindful that not everyone is naturally good at verbal communication, and it does require practice. Therefore, be gracious, stick it out, and learn this art together. I know one couple where the man was an exceptional communicator. He'd grown up in a very loving household, and he told his wife he loved her multiple times a day. His wife found this strange, as she had grown up differently. It took a few years of his patient 'coaching' to help her adapt to a verbal communication style that was more fitting for a loving relationship.

Treat verbal communication with courtesy and respect. Be humble. Show gratitude. Be objective, professional, and mature. Keep a gentle tongue. Avoid being sarcastic, sharp, critical, or mean. No swearing, no insults. While this may be later laughed off as 'blowing off steam,' the bitter words can linger long after the fight has been resolved. Words hold power, so be careful to use them respectfully.

Tip 2 – Written Communication

When I got married in the early '90s, mobile telephones did not exist. Kenny and I lived apart for one year due to my studies in Australia while he worked in Malaysia. International land-line telephone call rates were expensive. We had to visit our local post office to purchase letter sheets on which to write, then the sides were sealed (with saliva), and the letter posted off via 'snail mail.' It usually took about ten to fourteen days for our respective mail to arrive at the other end of the world. The great thing about this mode of communication is that his inner thoughts were shared in a manner that I have never observed elsewhere. I'm sure he witnessed a side of me that he'd never seen before too.

Have a go at writing a letter to each other and see whether this opens a whole new world of discovery and enriches your love and intimacy.

Tip 3 – Using Smart Devices

Communicating via text messages or online applications are instantaneous and fantastic. However, please be careful to write clearly and with courtesy. People think and express themselves differently, which leads to the risk that misunderstandings can occur because text messages may be read in a way that was not intended by the writer.

Keep text messages short and use many emojis to lighten the mood. Put oneself in the other person's shoes and imagine the reader's likely reaction. Smiling while texting can translate the heartfelt kindness, especially if the topic is subjective. Reread your text before hitting 'send' and if the subject matter is sensitive, let your draft message brew overnight prior to a final touch up before sending.

What to avoid: Writing when angry or writing anything negative. Don't read too quickly that you miss words and misconstrue the real intent.

These days, many young couples use text messages as an additional opportunity to flirt. Whilst there are some obvious risks (like sending the message to the wrong person, or a practical joke being misunderstood and becoming the subject of a complaint to the authorities), this can be a fun way to keep a marriage fresh. Of course, both parties should agree where to draw the line, as many people start out light and breezy until one party pushes things too far, and the other is left feeling like a killjoy. Work out boundaries and be very careful before you send anything that could cause potential harm to you or your reputation if the relationship sours or your phone is hacked. I've had more than one client whose partner threatened to leak potentially incriminating messages of their partner. So please proceed with caution!

I'd advise using text messages and emails for less sensitive and lighter subjects, and handle anything potentially difficult face-to-face. So instead of messaging, "I'm so furious with you right now. How dare you ..," it may be better to keep it short and say, "Hey, I'm pretty upset right now. I'd like to chat face-to-face. Can we make a time to talk later today?"

Tip 4 – Simple Rules

1. Out of respect and honour for your partner, whenever you're having a serious or heartfelt conversation (or a date), give your **undivided attention**. Put aside all electronic devices, reading, switch off the TV, and just be present and enjoy the moment. Husbands, give your wives your 100% focus and avoid pretending that you are listening when in fact your mind is elsewhere far away. Trust me, wives have sixth senses, and they will find out.

2. **Be gentle**, speak slowly, be light-hearted. Most couples are exhausted by nightfall and it's unwise to be misunderstanding and fighting instead of winding down to rest. Attend to complex issues or heavy discussions at pre-appointed times during the day. Wives, speak slowly and try not to share so many things at once. You don't have to speak out all your fifty thousand words quota for the day in the first ten minutes of your togetherness. Remember, it's regular communication often, not a massive dump of information or opening of the reservoir dam at one go!

3. Be an **active listener**. Be slow to speak, ask questions to encourage the conversation. Show interest and acknowledge by nodding and saying "uh-huh." Often, your partner may need a listening ear and is not expecting you to solve anything. Rick liked to fix things and his intermittent suggestions were interfering with the flow of his wife's sharing. He didn't understand why they were daily arguing

until I explained that his wife wanted to share and wanted him to listen and understand, nothing more.

4. Be considerate of your partner's circumstances. If you are constantly **interrupting** him while he is playing the guitar, or while she is planning her teaching course, or if he is in the midst of a gym workout, don't be surprised if you're told off. Be aware and wait for a mutually suitable time before broaching your desired topic for discussion.

5. **Be direct** and forthright. Say what you mean to say. Avoid speaking in riddles or beating around the bush. Don't make your partner guess what you are trying to say, as this can frustrate and damage the relationship.

Genuine Claim

"It has been ten years. He will not speak to me. He gives me the silent treatment every day, and I feel he does not acknowledge that I exist."

My Advice

Do not give up. There's always hope. Take baby steps in the right direction. Chip away slowly and consistently at the old huge brick wall because it will eventually crack open and break into small little pebbles. Start on the backfoot by saying something like, "When you ignore me for the whole week, I feel that you don't acknowledge that I exist, and I feel upset. I really want to know what is wrong. Can we talk about this?" But if your partner continually refuses to engage despite your best efforts, it's time to seek professional help. You can't go on living like this. You deserve better.

Genuine Claim

"Whenever I raise necessary issues to discuss, her responses provoke me to anger. I start yelling. She gets upset. We argue and fight every day. It seems hopeless."

My Advice

The fact that you are communicating is a sign of a healthy relationship. Unfortunately, you both need to learn a few tips to keep your conversations civil. Do not give up, but rather, put in the right efforts. Make a list of her responses that provoke you. Then gently tell her, "Honey, when you call me names and make threats, I get really scared, I'm sorry for yelling back, but that is my way of defending myself. Please forgive me. Can we both change the way we speak and say things differently so that we can remain calm and discuss as mature adults?"

Genuine Claim

"We are in love, but we speak different languages. How can we communicate effectively?"

My Advice

Be creative. There are many ways to communicate and not just verbally or in the same language. You can communicate through the eyes, using your hands, through meaningful touch, drawings.

MY SUGGESTIONS FOR YOUR ACTION

1. List down the ways you each communicate. What's working and what's not. Why?

2. List down how often you both communicate. Is this sufficient? Is it meaningful or superficial?

CHAPTER 5

MATTERS OF THE HEART
~ HONESTY ~

"Life isn't about waiting for the storm to pass; it's about learning how to dance in the rain."
Vivian Greene

I admit that being honest is probably one of the most difficult traits to practice. Honesty is important for living right and with a clear conscience. People sleep well after an honest day's work or feel triumphant from having done an honest deed. The ability to be honest stems from being secure in one's self and allowing others to speak freely even if their opinions are different. When views differ, agreeing to disagree, or disagreeing agreeably helps to preserve the peace. When it comes to marriage, honesty is one of the foundational stones for solidarity and longevity.

The Good Foundation of Honesty

I wonder how many couples practice honesty in their relationships. Honesty is like water that nourishes the grounds and keeps marriages green and lush. Where does one start? The answer lies with 'Me,' before I can expect any honesty out of 'We.'

It takes courage to be honest because it often leads to confrontation. Whether addressing a personal issue or having to deal with a problem, the risk of having to face up to an opponent who will react negatively rather than amicably may appear too huge. Most times, it is easier to avoid than to be honest.

In the past, I remember many instances when I was frustrated over one of Kenny's idiosyncrasies but instead of being honest about my feelings with him, I took the path of least resistance. Trust me when I share that the only person who suffered from my procrastination was me. Nowadays, when I notice that my peace is broken, I take a step back from the circumstances to survey the facts and details, have a thorough think of the best strategy to resolve the issue, then take action, lovingly, gently but firmly. O yes, I've also resorted to prayer, when my efforts alone did not yield any positive changes. My efforts have led to each of us having separate toothpaste tubes. His tube is oddly shaped from being squeezed indiscriminately and all over, while my tube is still in its original shape but slim, having been squeezed from the bottom up. He's learnt to ask me *before* throwing any household item away (he has previously thrown away an A4 sheet bearing all our account usernames and passwords, my friend's water bottle, another friend's sunglasses). I've learnt to let go instead of hoarding, much to Kenny's delight.

Learnt Behaviour

People learn honesty or dishonesty from the environment in which they grew up. Parents may inadvertently train their children to be dishonest and consequently spoil them when they allow children:

a. To give excuses for their erroneous ways.
b. To throw a tantrum or make a scene to win an argument.
c. To lie and wriggle out of a problem instead of holding them accountable.
d. To blame others for their wrongful actions, instead of teaching them to take responsibility and ownership for their actions.

When parents condone or acquiesce their children's bad attitudes or unacceptable behaviour to avoid the unpleasant confrontation, children learn that they can escape facing consequences when they create a scene. They will not experience the liberating feeling of being honest and transparent, they will not understand how to feel sorry and make amends, and their dishonesty will eventually become an entrenched character trait that will later have a detrimental impact on their marriage relationship.

Without the Honesty Make Up

When I work on divorce matters, what is glaring to me is the consistent lack of honesty within couples, even from the beginning. Whilst it's easy to judge, I think most of us can identify to some level. It's not intentional, but take for example in the early days, we're naturally on our best behaviour and present ourselves in the most flattering light. We may take extra time doing our hair and changing multiple outfits to find the best one. We may behave extra sweetly and jump to help at every opportunity. Unfortunately, over time we become complacent and take our partners for granted. The white lies gradually fade away. To be frank, this is natural and healthy. Most people will not allow a new date to hear them break wind, but I'm fairly certain that after some years into a relationship, most would admit having relaxed in this area. Just take care to avoid escalating into dishonesty at a higher level. A hidden medical or mental illness, a double life, an extra marital affair, spending the family's savings without notice or agreement.

The problem is that dishonesty tampers with trust. Initially, being in love automatically equates to, "I trust you completely." Unfortunately, when one is shifty, hides the truth and is later found out, the trust is instantaneously broken, and the guilty party faces an uphill climb to repair the broken trust and broken relationship. Often restoration is elusive and even impossible.

I know a beautiful, elderly man who cheated on his wife just once when he was in his mid-40s. He was weak and gave in to a moment of temptation. She never divorced him but chose to live separately from him. Thirty years later, he now lives in a retirement village and regularly visits her to show her his regret, love and devotion. He is making life-long amends by mowing her lawn and doing handywork around the house. She has never verbally forgiven him, yet clearly, they are still devoted to each other. She may have let pride rob her of what could have been a long, happy life together, because of one speed bump along the way. What a shame.

Marriages are precarious and sit on a shaky foundation when partners cannot live truthfully together.

Energy Sapper

Being dishonest can be exhausting. There is a constant need to live in secrecy, to cover up, to say one thing to Mr A while saying something different to Miss B, and then having to remember what was said to whom, to keep the different stories consistent between all involved. One can be smiling on the outside but scowling on the inside, appearing happy but seething over unresolved issues. It takes a lot of energy and effort to live this way. This involves mental gymnastics and doublemindedness. I cannot imagine anyone being truly happy living this type of life.

Sadly, many people make this a daily practice, although I hope that after reading this chapter, everyone would stop in their tracks and awaken to taking a stand to be truthful. Make efforts to become aware of yourself, and then of your partner, to discern whether you are each honest or otherwise, and then to make the necessary adjustments.

NOW *is* The Best Time

If you have not already done so, I encourage you NOW to take ownership of your internal moral infrastructure. Recognise character flaws to overcome, remove any deceit, observe any childish tendencies, and be true to yourself and to your partner.

Honesty is about:

- Being free from deceit or untruthfulness, being sincere, being genuine.
- Moral correctness, uprightness, integrity, ethics, principles, nobility, righteousness, right-mindedness, and upstandingness.

When couples live together knowing their partner is trustworthy, where there is no suspicion of motives or whereabouts, the relationship can be stable and secure.

Honesty in Me

The first place to start at is 'Me.' My relationship with 'Me' must be whole. I must love and accept 'Me.' I must develop a healthy self-esteem and understand my self-worth. The moment I am at peace with myself, I can begin to grow and develop and enjoy interaction with others from a place of honesty.

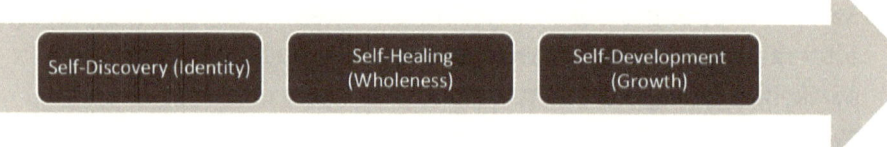

The steps in the process may interchange, but the best outcome is the peace, joy and energy experienced from the freedom of being authentic.

Over my career as a divorce lawyer, I have seen many marriages dissolve from a lack of personal awareness. Anna was thrilled by the high-flyer lifestyle that her husband promised her and fell madly in love with him. Regrettably, reality kicked in when she fell pregnant and gave birth to children one after another. Daily routine set in. She suddenly realised that her new value system as mother was not compatible with the ways her husband continued to live by, which was extravagant spending, flashy dressing, and pretentious conduct. The marriage broke down, and life for her became tough when she lost full access to his income. The saving grace for her was finding peace and happiness in living a genuine and honest life.

Jamie grew up under a domineering father who took firm control of the family's finances. When he married, he held all the family's income tightly, even the expenses and investments. This meant that his partner had nothing to her name and received minimal allowances for her expenditure. On the outside, this couple looked 'perfect' together; therefore, the breakup was unexpected and shocking to many. Even after counselling, Jamie continued to be in denial and struggled to overcome his paranoia and insecurities surrounding money and family finances, inbuilt from his childhood.

Robert grew up without a good male role model and panicked when his partner announced she was pregnant because he was not ready to assume fathering responsibilities. He smiled graciously at people's joyful congratulations, but internally he lacked the maturity and spent many nights crying out of fear. Fortunately, he sought counselling and managed to climb out of his inadequacies and insecurities with the support of his friends while also educating himself through books. His honesty with himself and everyone else saved his marriage.

Receive Other's Honesty

Invite your partner and others to give you constructive feedback about yourself. Ask them what they observe to be your strengths and weaknesses. Everyone has blind spots, but these may be obvious to other people who can shed light and share what areas in your life may need adjusting or change.

Early in my career, I had a client insist he was innocent of the charge of "harvesting lobsters without a license." When I received the police brief, the evidence stated that the patrol officer had found him on the back beach, in his drenched wetsuit and wearing a snorkel. The beach was covered with freshly caught lobsters, and there was no other person in sight. I started to prepare his 'not guilty' plea but was aided by my supervisor lawyer who had more experience and insight and steered me towards a different strategy for his defence, because he was *obviously not* 'not guilty'.

Phebe shared that early in her marriage, her husband regularly gave her honest feedback on unusual behaviours he observed. Once, he said she was unthoughtful because she'd make herself a cup of tea but never offered him one. He wasn't being malicious, and after he highlighted this habit, Phebe realised that it was because she'd grown up as the baby of her family; her older siblings and parents had doted upon her such that she hadn't developed that thoughtful nature. She received the constructive criticism and quickly addressed this side of her personality.

The truth can hurt. But in practising humility, letting go of pride and ego, and being teachable, receiving the honest caring comments of others may provide great benefit.

This goes both ways!

Sammy sincerely felt he was frugal, but his wife perceived him as Mr Scrooge. He was often upset when she purchased groceries for the family as he preferred a near empty refrigerator. He disagreed with spending money to buy presents or to celebrate special occasions. Through her honesty and his willingness to discuss (albeit on occasion it was confrontational and heated), Sammy gained understanding, changed his values, and developed a more generous attitude and greater consideration of others.

Wayne disagreed with his wife's desire to pursue further education which caused her to proceed without him being aware. She borrowed funds to pay the course fees, enrolled without his knowledge, and finally displayed the certificate of completion on the wall in the living room. He benefitted from her new employment income but never apologised for his earlier dismissive behaviour towards her. I can imagine a better way of discussion and decision making between Wayne and his wife, if only he was willing to allow honesty in the relationship.

Honesty About Your Partner

If you have a sixth sense telling you that something needs attention, stop and take heed. Don't ignore your gut feeling. Seek the counsel of trusted family and friends.

Fred's mother chose his wife for him. Out of respect for her, Fred did not protest and married her, even though there was a gnawing, uncomfortable feeling regarding his wife. Unfortunately, his wife turned out to be his worst nightmare, and his marriage was riddled with extreme stress and unrest. He found her to be dishonest, manipulative, and a drama queen when she wanted things to go her way. She finally abandoned Fred and their sons without any notice. Fred sought my help with the divorce and property settlement and was relieved when the proper restraints were put in place to prevent her being present or involved in his family life thereafter.

When One is Being Two-Faced

Many people behave one way inside the home and put on a façade when outside. Others act in such a way to 'save face,' then while at home and behind closed doors, they may behave immaturely, lose their temper, punch walls and destroy furniture when venting out their frustrations. Unfortunately, children who grow up watching this charade may learn hypocrisy and play this life game for themselves.

On the flip side, Rabbi Daniel Lapin (Lapin 2014) teaches the healthy version of this when he explains that the Hebrew word for face, "Panim," is a plural word, and the proper saying is actually, "if you wish to know me, look at my faces." He explains that Panim is never singular, and one never says, "look at my face." In fact, everyone is multi-faced because of the different hats worn throughout the day, depending on what roles one assumes at different times during the day. In my case as an example, in a typical day, I would wear the following different faces:

1. In the morning, the face of homemaker, wife, and mum, ensuring breakfast is prepared and consumed, and chores and homework are completed before everyone heads out of the house for school and work. My face is patiently waiting for Kenny to finish his leisurely sweep of leaves from off the driveway, even though I need to quickly drive out of the garage to head towards the office.

2. During office hours, I wear the face of lawyer and put on different faces when interacting with colleagues, interviewing clients, or dealing with opposing lawyers.

3. In the evening, my face is that of coach to couples while discussing their relationships.

4. Finally, before I lay my head to sleep, I wear a humble and grateful face in prayer to God.

In this sense, I am not being 'two-faced,' which is an English phrase with negative connotations, but rather behaving appropriately according to the circumstances. There is nothing dishonest about this.

It is important for every couple to understand this, so that partners wear the right face at the right time. I know of a father who forgot to switch his managerial face to the loving caring face while at home with the family, and his overly authoritarian disposition ended up hurting more than nurturing his relationship with his wife and children.

When Not to Be Honest

There are many ways to say the same thing. Sometimes being tactful and exercising wisdom is more important than blurting out the truth and causing hurt out of ignorance. Be careful not to cause offence by your honesty.

For example, saying, "Hey, your breath stinks," even though it is true, could shock a well-intentioned husband who is reaching out to plant a loving kiss. The alternative, more gracious expression could be, "Honey, your breath is a little strong after eating garlic for dinner. Please brush your teeth or have a few Tic Tacs first." Another example could be avoiding the obvious, "You've let yourself become sluggish and lazy" but instead saying, "I'd really like for both of us to clean up our diets and start exercising. I want us both to live long, happy lives together. What exercises could we do together?"

Steps to Honest Living

A marriage requires constant positive effort to achieve daily and ongoing success. Allowing honest sharing may cause whatever is hidden and blocking the marriage success to surface and be dealt with. Honesty can right the wrongs, repair the broken and restore what was lost. It may be the spark that ignites the relationship engine towards an enthusiastic adventurous ride forward.

Firstly, have a think about what is 'not quite right,' but has been ignored because it requires effort to correct.

Write down your responses to the three points below.

1. Identify all the areas of your life that require attention. For example:

- Every morning I awake feeling lethargic.
- My back is in constant pain.
- My income is insufficient to meet expenses.

2. Identify areas in your relationship that are troubling you. For example:
    - I suspect he is flirting with younger women through online dating websites.
    - I feel it's unfair when she keeps her income for herself but expects all my income to be used to support the family.
    - He doesn't help with any chores and ignores the kids.

3. Identify idiosyncrasies that frustrate you or steal your peace. For example:
    - He constantly makes a loud guttural noise while clearing his throat.
    - She brought a dog home without prior discussion or notice, then expects me to accommodate her decision, even though she knows that I don't fancy dogs.
    - Her whole attention is given to the newborn baby, and I feel neglected and ostracised.

Secondly, confront the issues with love, open-mindedness, a listening ear to understand and agree on the appropriate solutions.

These attitudes are not going to be helpful and must cease:

- Pretending that everything is okay when it is not.

- Denying the truth of the circumstances.
- Making excuses for the situation in attempt to sugar-coat or deflect the attention to something else.

Be transparent. Be vulnerable. Be willing to face reality. Ask questions to seek clarification and gain understanding. It takes courage, but it is well worth the effort.

Thirdly, cultivate a culture and an environment of honesty. It may have to start with you, and then allow the ripple effect to gain momentum. Prepare a family meal and take turns sharing, "What was the best thing that happened to you today?" Then, "What was the worst part of your day?"

If you have children, be daring enough to ask their feedback with, "Is there anything that Mum and Dad are doing that makes you unhappy?" and let them speak freely. Quash your reactionary conduct. Take notes. Then adjust your conduct towards them. I guarantee that relationally, things will improve significantly from then on.

Fourthly, resolve with the best solution. Act positively. Be creative. Be resourceful. Do what it takes to make amends and reconcile.

A vision of a couple who have honest communication and a healthy relationship may be when they are both outgoing, very comfortable and secure. They may express joy on their faces and carry themselves well, with a lot of energy coming out with them. You can tell that they have communication that is honest and transparent, and they are comfortable being vulnerable with each other. That is the best relationship that one can aim to have. Avoid aiming to be the 'perfect-looking' couple, rather, aim to put your house in order. Your house being your inner self, your relationship with your partner, and your relationship with your family members. This peaceful state brings great contentment and bliss.

Genuine Claim

"I cannot bring myself to ask my husband for money, even though my mother is ill, and I want to fly home to be with her. He will throw a tantrum and threaten to divorce me. He wants me around to cook him dinner every night."

My Advice

Pluck up the courage to speak your honest feelings. Be gentle but strategic. Share how your mother has benefitted your family with her babysitting, her cooking, her love and many gifts. Then share your fears that this may be the last opportunity for you to spend time with your mum and that she needs your support and help. Speak to him in a way that he can understand. Request that he refrains from being angry as it is unnecessary and hurtful. Explain the details of the trip, such as dates for departure and return, where you will spend most of your time and the costs. Offer to prepare dinners for freezing so that he can simply heat up and consume, which removes any inconvenience for him.

Genuine Claim

"I suspect that my husband is keeping a secret from me because of his strange behaviour. I hope he is not having an affair."

My Advice

Ask him outright, "Are you having an affair? Is there another woman?" Listen to his response, but also observe his body language and discern if he is telling the truth or not. Discover whether he is truthful or being deceitful. Seek the help of a trusted friend or counsellor.

MY SUGGESTIONS FOR YOUR ACTION

1. Be honest with yourself. Take notice of your thoughts.

    a. Make a list of what you love and appreciate about yourself, and what you do not.

    b. Discover your identity, bolster your weakness, continue learning and growing.

2. Invest in coaches who can enhance various areas of your life, such as:

    a. A relationship coach (communication and intimacy).

    b. A diet coach (nutrition and energy levels).

    c. A fitness coach (stamina and strength).

    d. A business coach (productivity and revenue).

CHAPTER 6

WHICH BUTTONS TO PUSH
~ LOVE LANGUAGES ~

"The best love is the kind that awakens the soul and makes us reach for more, that plants a fire in our hearts and brings peace to our minds. And that's what you've given me. That's what I'd hope to give you forever."
Nicholas Sparks

When Kenny and I married, we were wildly in love. But I must say that we were madly arguing too. It seemed that we kept pressing the wrong buttons. It was like we spoke two completely different languages. I sometimes felt like I was from earth and Kenny was from a galaxy not yet discovered. We weren't from different planets, but two parallel universes! After his work, Kenny would spend excess time cleaning the house, tidying the yard and preparing dinner. In his mind, that was how he showed me he loved me. But I didn't receive it that way. By the time I got home from work, he was exhausted from all the physical exertion and had nothing left to give. This made me feel unimportant. I couldn't give two hoots if the lawn was mown and the potted plants fertilised. Whereas, to show Kenny I loved him, I tended to share with him everything about my day to make him feel included, but this made Kenny feel irritable. He just wanted to hear me comment on the work he'd done.

Eventually, through study and reflection, we came to learn that we both gave and received love in different ways. Neither of us was right or wrong, we were just wired differently. In order to communicate our love effectively, we had to adjust our expectations and learn a new style.

I wonder why this is so. Is there a mystery? Or a reasonable explanation for why such a dichotomy exists for couples in love? Wouldn't it be great to have your actions acknowledged by your partner? Can you imagine communicating with your partner without experiencing any arguments, and interactions are satisfying and meaningful? How wonderful would marriages be when partners understand, appreciate, and respect each other!

The Five Love Languages

Dr Gary Chapman describes the following five main ways of communicating love in his book *The Five Love Languages* (Chapman 1992).

Love Language	How people characteristically communicate their Love Language	In practical terms
Words of affirmation	People use words to affirm others.	"Darling, you give me strength." "You are such a loving dad to the children."
Acts of service	Showing love through actions.	"I show my love by working hard to earn income for the family." "I show my love by tending the garden and making it beautiful."
Receiving gifts	Some people feel loved when they receive a gift.	"I feel loved when you surprise me with gifts that are meaningful to me."
Quality time	Giving the other person focused attention.	"I feel loved when you put the newspaper away to chat with me during my coffee break."
Physical touch	Love expressed through appropriate touch.	"I feel loved when you make the effort daily to kiss and hug me upon leaving the house and arriving home."

Love Bank Check-Up

Every person has a love bank that needs to be filled with regular deposits. There is an innate need to love and be loved. If we know how to maintain a healthy fill of our own love bank, we can give out of this resource and receive without embarrassment. The effective practice of expressing and receiving love enhances relationships. The knowledge of the various love languages will assist our efforts to be effective in communicating love, because every person is unique in how they show and desire love.

In relationships, the 'love' that endures over time and through all sorts of circumstances must be intentional, purposeful, and not just romantic. The expression of love transcends personalities, background cultures, and if communicated properly, can have a hugely positive impact on the recipient. Any person who feels significant, worthy, and celebrated will flourish, blossom and be encouraged to achieve greatness in life. Partners must understand this phenomenon and properly fuel their partner's love bank by communicating in their partner's love language.

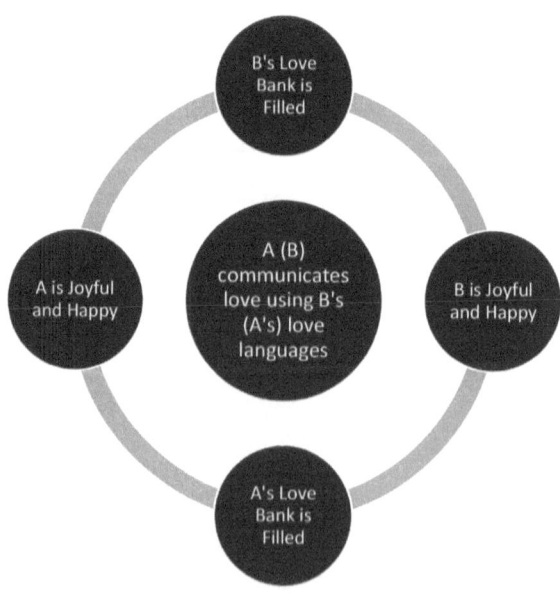

Which Buttons to Push

You will experience breakthroughs in your marriage relationship the moment you understand the different love languages, recognise the cues and signals, and speak the love language of your partner.

Words of Affirmation

People with words of affirmation as their love language express their love verbally, for example:

> "You should sing more, because your voice is incredible."
>
> "I love how you stand up for the underdog."
>
> "Thank you for being protective of me."
>
> "You look like James Bond in that suit! Wow!"
>
> "Our kids are so lucky to have you as their mum."
>
> "That dinner was incredible, you're such a good cook."
>
> "I love the way you make our place so homely."
>
> "Thank you for always mowing the lawn without asking. You're the best!"

This sort of encouragement is like a stamp of approval to one's partner. It may boost one's confidence to dream bigger, achieve more than initially imagined, and bring stability into tumultuous circumstances (such as loss of a loved one). It may even draw out buried abilities to be used for the benefit of many.

Couples who take each other for granted and let days, weeks, even months pass by without affirming each other allow their love to dry up and die. Even if this is not your love language, I would encourage you to show love through saying something positive and encouraging to your partner daily. Let this practice become 'automatic' until a good habit is formed.

Do this exercise as often as possible:

a. Look into your heart and find the source of love and kindness (LOVE).

b. Consider all the good actions and efforts of your partner and all the benefits s/he brings (THOUGHTS).

c. Convert your love and thoughts into positive words and practice saying these to your partner (ACTION).

d. Find many opportunities to speak affirmingly to your partner (ACTION).

Now observe your partner's transformation because you have regularly and generously showered him/her with affirming words. These positive expressions will soon become a natural habit. Obviously, it needs to be sincere for this to become automatic over time. But remember not to let phrases like "you legend" or "awesome superstar" become a meaningless colloquial saying and your over-enthusiasm appear fake. Yes, there is a fine balance. But the best part is knowing that it's difficult for anyone to be angry at you when you're constantly heaping praise upon them.

Acts of Service

People with this love language feel loved when they notice their partner doing something for them.

It is important to share with your partner what you would like him or her to do for you, and then follow up with kind words of appreciation or gratitude. If you know your partner is doing handy work around the house out of his love for you, don't just keep the love to yourself. Be sure to take notice and say "thank you." It is important to verbalise the love upon each other! Similarly, if you

Which Buttons to Push

notice your wife cooking up your favourite dish out of her love for you, freely compliment and encourage her efforts.

Jerry was feeling unappreciated and unimportant because his wife did not verbally express her appreciation of him. She was pregnant and had constant midnight food cravings. Out of commitment and love, he'd get out of bed, get dressed, and drive to the store to buy whatever she craved. His love language was acts of service, and he was willing to make sacrifices out of love, but he needed to hear her words of affirmation which unfortunately were not forthcoming. He often felt sleepy at work and gradually became resentful and emotionally withdrawn from his wife. One day, he took notice of his work colleague, who was vivacious and flirtatious towards him, who freely praised him and overtly complimented his achievements. Before the baby was born, Jerry had left his wife and taken off on a new relationship with his work colleague. Not being acknowledged for loving acts creates a love deficit, which cultivates fertile ground for temptation to take root and germinate into undesirable and negative consequences. In this story, Jerry's work colleague's flattery and positive words filled his void and made her seem extremely attractive to him.

Because it does not cost very much to do so, recognise the love that underpins acts of service and express positive words in acknowledgement and appreciation as often as possible.

Receiving Gifts

If you know that your partner's love language is that of receiving gifts, learn to be thoughtful and give meaningful gifts. Plan a special occasion to surprise her/him with your gift. You may need to research or ask trusted friends for their input. Gifts have the power to melt the hardest hearts and encourage love to permeate any barren atmosphere. Giving and receiving gifts will go a long way to fan the love flame and keep it burning continuously!

People with this love language will often drop non-intentional clues about gifts they'd like. Start being a proactive listener, and as soon as you hear the words "one day I'd love to get one of those," or "I really need this thing," make a note of it subtly on your phone. Then, later when you're stuck for gift ideas, you can simply fish out the list and buy something your partner actually wants. They will be so impressed that you listened and remembered!

Quality Time

People whose love language is quality time will indirectly 'say' the following:

- "I feel like you are always too busy for me."
- "We don't spend enough time together alone."
- "I need more time with just you and no distractions."

It is worthwhile finding out what type of 'quality time' satisfies your partner. A husband may feel that quality time occurs while watching football together, cycling, or taking long drives in the country. The wife, on the other hand, may prefer sitting by the fireplace and cuddling, or sipping coffee at a nearby café. Learning your partner's love language will enable your marriage to prosper!

Helpful tips for those whose partner's love language is 'quality time.'

- Stay present and focused.
- Be relaxed and enjoy the moment.
- Avoid multi-tasking by squeezing in work to this time, taking work calls, making mental plans for future activities, or catching up on social media.
- Daydreaming or falling asleep does not count.

If you're too tired to concentrate, let your partner know and request a rain check on this time together. Sometimes, one partner may agree to an activity like going for a walk with their partner to spend quality time together, but then complain along the way and protest that they actually didn't want to go. Complaining or looking bored negates the kindness of agreeing to spend quality time together. Once you have agreed to invest into the activity, be engaged, make it mutually enjoyable. Grinning and bearing will only nullify your good intentions.

Physical Touch

Appropriate touch such as greeting with a hug and a kiss, holding hands when you go for walks, sitting beside each other close enough for shoulders and arms to touch, are all a means of communicating love. This is deeply meaningful to the one whose love language is physical touch.

Remember, sexual activity is just one expression of the many ways to express love through physical touch. Even a soothing massage, a gentle backrub, or practising your amateur reflexology techniques on your partner are valid ways to satisfy this love language!

Miscommunication

Max's internal dialogue: "My love language is acts of service and I show my love for you by keeping the house in tip-top shape. I am constantly looking out to see what needs fixing or putting in order. But nothing I do seems to make you happy. Why does pleasing you have to be so difficult?"

Audrey's internal dialogue: "My love language is quality time and I feel loved when you sit on the couch with me and just chat. Why do you have to be so busy around the house? I feel that you are distracted and distant and our love has grown cold."

Audrey can see that Max takes good care of the handy work around the house but has failed to acknowledge and affirm his actions of love towards her. This will cause Max to feel unappreciated and unloved. Max does not make deposits into Audrey's love bank, because there is a never-ending number of tasks to do around the house, and he cannot sit still until all of it is completed (which is never!) The status quo left unchecked may spiral the relationship into a ravine of dissatisfaction. The moment Audrey starts acknowledging Max's work, he will feel loved, and she could be making huge deposits into his love bank by saying:

- "Thank you for fixing the leak in the tap. That's a big help!"
- "I noticed you got a second remote for the garage door which I can keep in my car!"
- "You are a champ for doing the dishes after every meal!"

Audrey's love language is 'quality time,' and she enjoys sitting by the fireplace, sipping tea, having a chat about the highs and lows of the day. She could regularly remind Max what her love language is and say:

- "Thanks for doing the dishes, Babe, I really appreciate it. Can we sit on the couch and chat? Remember, my love language is quality time, and I just need ten minutes of your undivided attention. I promise I won't talk your ear off! But I do want to hear about your day!"
- "Do you want to watch our favourite TV show together now? Remember my love language is physical touch, and I just need to cuddle up in your arms for a while."
- "Wanna shower together after you do the dishes?" (for double satisfying of quality time and physical touch).

Be a Jack of All Trades with Love Languages

Once you start speaking the love language of your partner, the floodgates of romance will gradually open due to the constant deposits into your partner's love bank. The synergy and chemistry will grow. The results will be phenomenal.

We can all communicate our love through speaking affirmingly and positively to our partner and loved ones by performing acts of service, giving presents, investing quality time, and by appropriate touching. We can all look forward to an adventurous life with our partners and even our loved ones through the conscious practice of all five love languages. Armed with this knowledge, your marriage will be a winner!

Finally, I'd also like to say that as humans, we are bestowed with a full set of emotions for a reason. Being proficient with exercising love languages does not mean you must be always happy. Being sad, mad, frustrated are not inherently 'bad emotions.' There are times and places that these negative emotions are completely healthy and ought to be expressed properly. These can enhance the marriage relationship, especially when embraced together with the exercise of love languages.

Genuine Claim

"I did not experience a positive upbringing and am not familiar with expressing or receiving love."

My Advice

Expressing love, giving, and receiving love is a learned behaviour. You are not alone. Every person goes through a learning curve to discover and practice expressing and receiving love. Some curves are steeper than others, but so long as you are open and teachable, you can research, read, and put in the effort to make this way of life become second nature.

Genuine Claim

"I feel that my partner is cold and aloof towards my efforts to show love to him. Sometimes, I feel that my love backfires and my efforts are wasted. I just can't do it anymore."

My Advice

Please do not give up. May I suggest that you gently explain to him the motivation for your actions. For example, say this:

> "Honey, I've cooked your favourite lasagne. When you don't say 'thank you', or you keep silent, I am unsure whether you appreciate my efforts or not. Can you give me a hug and tell me how good the food tastes because that will mean a lot to me?"

Your partner may be oblivious and ignorant and may be taking you for granted. In fact, many partners are in the same boat. Providing explanation will shed light and provide clarity, and this ties back to the importance of good communication skills. Hopefully, it will draw out the right response from your partner. Tell him how you feel, gently and respectfully, then reconcile and resolve. Go one step further and discover your partner's love language. Become fluent in it to fill up his love bank.

Genuine Claim

"I can't love my partner because she has deeply offended me. I hate her."

My Advice

I empathise with your feelings, but venture to say that the hateful feelings or resentfulness is in fact GOOD! 'Hate' really means that you still have feelings for your partner, and in fact is unrequited love! It results from the love you have for your partner that has been deeply offended.

May I advise you to make time to be completely alone. Find space where you can be by yourself and free from distractions. Work through why you are offended and how your partner has offended you. Decide to forgive, then let go of the offence and hatred. Wipe the slate clean and start again. Find the love that is deeply embedded in you and magnify this love to be bigger than your offence. Forgiveness is the key to breakthrough.

Find someone you trust or a relationship coach to help you through this period. When you are ready, speak with your partner to work out how to stop the cycle of offending, bitterness, and hate. Re-focus with speaking your love languages and experience the amazing results of a successfully renewed relationship.

MY SUGGESTIONS FOR YOUR ACTION

1. Click on this link to take this online survey and discover your love language: http://www.5lovelanguages.com then compare your results with your partner.

2. Read *The Five Love Languages* by Dr Gary Chapman.

CHAPTER 7

TAMING ANGRY HIPPOS
~ RESOLVING CONFLICT ~

"The first to apologize is the bravest. The first to forgive is the strongest. The first to forget is the happiest."
Unknown

In the movie *My Big Fat Greek Wedding* (Gold Circle Films 2002), Ian Miller fell in love with Toula, and head over heels into the loud, chaotic family relations of the Greek Portokalis family. There were scenes of in-your-face confrontations, loud parties, and constant chatter during gatherings. Toula's dad Gus could not understand why Ian's parents were so frustratingly "dry .. like biscuit", even though they were obviously British and therefore characteristically reserved. The movie depicted the undesirability of conflict, but because the Greeks always confronted issues by open and amicable discussion, the relationships worked out beautifully in the end.

Conflict is Guaranteed

If you expect that your marriage will start romantically and continue in bliss indefinitely, your bubble may quickly burst and your exit out of La La Land may be sudden! In all honesty, so long as two people are doing life together, conflict will occur, sometimes more and sometimes less, simply because:

a. People are different in gender, age, and personality, and raised in different backgrounds, culture, education, and life experiences.

b. They have formed different values and have different ambitions and desires.

c. They hold to different perspectives and opinions.

d. We all experience tiredness, illness and get hangry (hungry and angry), even succumbing to hormonal issues like PMS and menopause.

Amidst the love and chemistry, sparks are bound to fly and clashes will lead to conflict. Inevitably the person(s) closest to you tend to cop the most damage when as Forrest Gump legendarily said "sh*t happens". This is the 'gift' of proximity. Therefore, expect conflict, be comfortable with conflict, and the best favour you can do for yourself is to learn how to handle it!

Grounds for Conflict

Men and women are different. Period! That's the biggest ground for conflict.

Other grounds for conflict include:

1. Inadequate communication.
2. Stress from life's routine.
3. Pressure to earn income.
4. Differing parenting styles.
5. The lack of trust.
6. Abuse (could be physical, financial, emotional, verbal, social, sexual, spiritual).
7. The in-laws.
8. Health.
9. Mental issues.
10. Major events (causing trauma).

Cease Living Blind

Without the knowledge and skills to resolve conflict, couples can experience a merry-go-round of negative experiences being repeated. No wonder some people give up. The good news is that by learning the tools for conflict resolution, the quest for a happy life together can become a reality!

Avoid Creating Conflict Out of Ignorance

Many conflict situations can be prevented if one partner is aware of the other's personality.

When we first started out, I used to return home tired from work but excited to share with Kenny everything about my day. I was oblivious to his tiredness from his long day at work and his need for quiet to stare into space for a few (long) moments. (By the way,

I observe this to be a 'guy' thing, and this tendency may appear in sons too, so you've been forewarned to be patient with your sons). He'd listen to my passionate and oratorial speech out of love for me, but quickly float off to somewhere like planet Jupiter because of his inability to focus, while continuing to nod in agreement (even when there was nothing to agree to). The evening started out 'loving' but ended up with two exasperated persons. Unfortunately, it took a few repeats of this scene before we each spoke up and wised up.

We've learnt to allow each other solo downtime to relax and refresh at the time of day when energy is at its lowest level, then later come together for a hearty meal and mutual engagement. A hungry partner may be grumpy, and growl like a bear, be irritable and unreasonable. Let the tummy receive the yummy calories it craves first before anything else.

If your wife acts unusually out of character and irrational, don't bite back. Stop and think for a minute, "is this your wife speaking? Or is it the time of the month for her?" Decide to shower love upon her for a day and see if her mood dramatically improves after twenty-four hours.

Also, don't underestimate the healing power of a long dip in the bathtub to wash away all the agitation from a stressful day. Guys have been observed to have 'the time of the month' too and sometimes he may be snappy because of a challenging work project.

Must It Only Be Your Way?

In some relationships, the breadwinner calls the shots and can be high-handed, controlling, and unreasonable. The homemaker, on the other hand, may have little or no say in the decision making because her work is perceived to be of any tangible cash value. Such one-sided power control may be seen to be abusive, emotionally and even financially. Equally, the wife may think all child-related decisions are a woman's domain and dismiss her husband's opinion.

Notably, for the purposes of assessing what contributions were made to the matrimonial pool of assets, the Family Court in Australia may attribute a monetary value to homemaker duties, and depending on the duties performed all day long for seven days in the week, the value could be a six figure number!

Some people use the loudest volume to have the last say. In such circumstances, the conclusion was reached but not from equal opportunity to contribute, and neither would it have been mutual nor amicable.

For couples to make decisions together, there should be a willingness to hear the other person's point of view and reach a reasonable compromise or joint agreement.

When There Are No Rules

Conflict can be ugly, scary, unpleasant, even horrible. Especially if the philosophy is 'free for all' and 'anything goes' and there is no requirement for restraint or self-control.

The couple who does not practice respect for the other person or property may express anger, hurt and frustration in various extreme forms such as screaming, pushing, pulling, throwing, and breaking of household items. Threats and accusations are hurled like javelin with intent to hurt. Usually, such actions are destructive and may cause damage to the relationship. Any involvement of the police may lead to court action or criminal charges being issued.

If this is you, I advise you to calm down and get off from your high horse. Have a look at yourself in the mirror. You are capable of behaving in a manner much better than this.

Play by the Rules

Theoretically, it is easy to tell couples to be loving, kind, and courteous during conflict situations. In practice, in the heat of the moment, all guns come out firing and daggers are thrown indiscriminately. Who will win this fight? Words like cannonballs are hurled from the depths of passion, together with spears and arrows, aiming to strike the bullseye hard.

Do you think couples could fight as though they are playing Swamp Football? There are rules for the twelve players who play in the mud, throw or kick mud around, and after competing for twenty-six minutes, there are little or no injury or deaths. Couples can engage in conflict fairly and squarely, but there must be rules for the conduct and engagement, because ignorance or non-application of these rules may cause the marriage to breakdown and the family members to become casualties of foul play.

Sometimes having a think about what life would be like **without** one's partner may help bring perspective and self-restraint. There is nothing wrong with speaking the truth. However, the truth is best spoken in love. Avoid causing injury to the other party and potentially destroying the relationship. Hurt takes time to repair, so why would you behave in such a way as to cause injury, and then suffer the costs of repair? That sounds like self-sabotage! Therefore, make some rules about what conduct is acceptable and what is out-of-line. If you must fight, try to be civil and let each other come out intact, and even better, enriched, through the experience!

Resolve Conflict Properly

Address issues but allow equal opportunity to present individual viewpoints. Keep in mind that the conclusion must be resolution, reconciliation, and peace. Watch out if one feels scarred, estranged, or embittered.

I have met clients who reside at rehabilitation centres for a period and learn a way of life to overcome and avoid further abuse of substances. Some of them had felt overwhelmed after suffering traumatic conflict with their partners and took to drink or drugs. Others suffered other forms of trauma. Unfortunately, taking refuge in substances provides temporary relief and may not be an effective solution to the problems.

Helen was exasperated with her partner because he preferred to drown his frustration by playing computer games all night long and ignoring her and the children. He just didn't want to face her or discuss their issues. He lacked the practical skills needed to resolve difficulties, so he simply avoided.

Diving into other activities may serve as a distraction or a band-aid covering up the problem at hand. When the momentary soothing wears off, the issues may eventually catch up to you. Hence, it's best to confront and resolve asap, rather than procrastinate and divert your attention to other things. If you are overwhelmed by the conflict with your partner, you could seek professional help. It may take some effort and work, but you should know that there is light at the end of the tunnel.

Communication Skills

The ones who master the skills for effective communication will enjoy great joy and contentment in their marriage. Miscommunications and misunderstandings are the main causes of conflict and the catalyst for relationships to breakdown.

One of my clients lost his marriage after five years. He had two young children whom he loved deeply. His daily arguments with his wife became mega shouting matches, and finally, the wife called on the help of the police to evict him from the matrimonial home. He now lives with his parents while she is living as a single parent with the children. They both still love each other but are too battle-scarred to attempt reviving their marriage.

The table below depicts a typical conversation that starts out well with good intentions but eventually becomes pear-shaped.

	Words actually spoken	**Actual intention but not spoken**
H	"Honey, I want to have the kids on Friday night."	I want to spend more time with the kids because I miss them so much.
W	"No, because Mary (daughter) is not ready to see you."	I miss you being nice to me and before we discuss your time with the kids, I want you to say something nice to make me feel good. I'm referring to Mary but in fact am hoping that you'll notice me.
Notes	They are speaking, but are failing to communicate directly and clearly what they each intend or want.	

	Words actually spoken	**Actual intention but not spoken**
H	"Just a month ago, we were all happily living together. Now I only see the kids for a few hours each Sunday and that's too little time for me."	I really miss being with you and the kids daily. Can we try again to make the family life work?
W	"Too bad. That's not my problem. Mary is not ready."	Be nice to me and I'll reciprocate being nice to you with more time with the kids.
	Both parties are now tired and frustrated. Neither is saying what they mean. Neither is hearing the real intentions behind the spoken words. Neither is getting their needs met. The husband wants more time with the kids. The wife wants the husband to show her love.	
H	"You are being unreasonable and difficult. Mary loves me and will want to spend time with me."	Why are you playing this game and making it impossible for me to see the kids?
W	"You don't understand. You are impossible. I'll make sure you don't get to see the kids at all!"	If you can't show me love, then I'll be mean to you too and prevent your access to the kids.
H	"You *#!^@. How dare you?"	There you go again, threatening to take the kids away from me. The kids are my whole world. I live for the kids. I work to get income for my kids. I am nothing without the kids.

	Words actually spoken	**Actual intention but not spoken**
W	"You don't deserve to see the kids. You are a &#!^@. Have you been drinking? Why do you always have to be violent and threatening?"	I am scared whenever you start yelling because I fear you might hit me and hurt me. I don't trust you because in the past you didn't control yourself.
	The wife has threatened to prevent his access to the kids whom he loves dearly. He is fearful of her power and this triggers his anger which he expresses out of a defensive stance, by raising his voice and swearing at her. The wife is fearful of the husband's power from his greater physical size and louder manly voice. She reacts with aggression and uses his past addiction to alcohol as a weapon to hit him. She has touched on a sore spot, despite his changed behavior from long ago.	
	He swears even more and motions to hit her, even though he never intends to touch her. The wife reacts by hitting him first. However, she is viewed by the police as the victim and needing protection. She is after all only five feet tall, whereas he is over six feet tall. Finally, the police attends at the property and removes him from the property.	

May I suggest the following advice:

a. Avoid making your partner guess what you really want to say.

Because:

- b. Your partner is not a mind reader and has not been trained to decipher the hidden meanings and intentions behind your words.
- c. S/he may not be ready (too tired, stressed, anxious) to play this mind-reading game with you.
- d. They will more likely understand a whole lot better if you say what you mean to say and are clear, direct and forthright. Do not be vague or use ambiguities.

Wholeness in Yourself

To effectively handle and resolve conflict, it's imperative to be whole within yourself; body, mind and soul. When there are issues in a relationship, it's often because people aren't tuned in or knowledgeable about themselves, let alone their partner. Conflict is exacerbated by such actions as pushing, shoving, punching the wall, and lashing out at each other. In contrast, those who are more mature and secure in themselves will more likely work to settle the conflict by holding a tempered discussion.

Be mutually patient and longsuffering while still learning the relationship tricks of the trade.

Find out which of the following is your likely reaction or response to conflict.

When confronted with a problem, your adrenalin charges up and you **FIGHT** back, retaliate, lash out. Could be for self-protection, or to dominate, out of anger or rage. This is an offensive mode.	When confronted with a problem, you take **FLIGHT**, run away, quit. For self-protection, self-preservation, out of fear. You need time and space to plan and process how to win. This is a defensive mode.
You are a **CONFRONTER**. You charge towards the problem.	You are an **AVOIDER**. You ignore, withdraw, retreat, and pretend nothing has occurred because you want to keep the peace.
The **BULL** approach. You see 'red' and go for the target with all your might.	The **TORTOISE** approach. You hide your head in your shell and hope the problem goes away by itself.

There is no right or wrong way to deal with conflict. However, self-awareness is necessary because our behaviour may need to change to achieve the outcome.

For example, if the 'fight' person makes the conflict personal and seeks revenge through, say, physical or financial means, it will be necessary for him/her to change if he/she wishes to repair the broken trust and expect the partner to respond positively again. If the 'flight' person refuses to deal with the obvious character flaw, then she may have to seek professional help to prevent shipwreck of the marriage.

Take Pro-Active Steps

Some couples endure the other's idiosyncrasies and unacceptable habits just to keep the peace and avoid confrontation. Unfortunately, the resentment can build up to such an extent that the pressure cracks the fortress walls of the relationship, and the previously cute and tolerable behaviour becomes an offence greater than the unforgivable sin. Imagine the consequences of negative emotions flaring up and the unjust treatment of each other, causing the relationship to spiral downwards into a deep dark valley. Sadly, the offending party is usually oblivious of the other's suffering because the victim chose to remain silent instead of making the effort to bring up the problem for attention and resolving.

Couples can better handle problems by cultivating the same values and rules, such as the following:

a. Agree to create a culture where one can raise any issue openly without fear of repercussions.
b. Be pro-active and request a time for discussion.
c. Agree not to be judgemental but listen to gain understanding.
d. Agree not to take it as a personal attack, but rather, tackle the issue together.

I know it can feel unfamiliar and uncomfortable, but as you pluck up the courage to try and practice this restorative type of resolving issues, the openness and objectivity in the mutually agreed approach will become second nature. You may even discover that you welcome and enjoy the confrontation! It is extremely satisfying for each partner to observe the other's maturity in this.

Proper Communication

Best to say what's on your mind and what you are feeling. If you can't verbalise this, then put pen to paper and write it all down. Don't forget to include your suggestions for the solutions to the problem. Best to avoid procrastinating in communicating your complaint to your partner because each day has its own challenges, and many small issues accumulated can grow into an insurmountable mountain of problems too huge and complex to manage when it finally surfaces or explodes.

Be clear, direct, and to the point, with what you consider to be wrong.

For example, you are feeling cold because your partner has just walked in through the front door and left it open, such that the wind draft is blowing directly at you.	
Right way of speaking to your partner:	Outcome:
"Honey, I'm feeling cold because there is a breeze blowing directly at me through the open door. Would you please close the door behind you?"	Partner shuts the door. You are happy, your partner is happy. The evening progresses on a positive note.

Wrong way of speaking to your partner:	Outcome:
You: "Honey, do you think the room is cold?" Partner: "Really? I don't feel cold at all." You: "You can't feel the breeze? Are you serious? You must be thick-skinned."	Your partner is unsuspecting and lacks insight into your unspoken thoughts. He is honest in his response. He is oblivious to how you are feeling because you have not told him. He gets offended. You get upset. The tiny issue gets blown up into misunderstandings and bad temper. The good evening turns sour.

For heaven's (and every couple's) sake, avoid saying what you do not mean and simply say what you really mean.

Watch the Filters

People have filters in their minds through which they process what is heard. Mr A may say "X" but Mrs B hears "XXX." He may have said, "I don't like spicy food", but she hears instead, "He hates my cooking and does not love me." Her presumption leads to her becoming hurt by his short, unqualified remark even though he didn't mean that at all! Her filter of self-consciousness and insecurity has negatively influenced what she heard.

A conversational skill to practice is to ask the receiving partner to repeat what was heard to ensure both understand what is said and heard.

Person A: "XYZ."

Person B: "Did you mean XYZ?"

Person A: "Yes, I meant XYZ."

Regular practice of this 'mirror' talk will put conflict out of business.

Be clear about what the fight is over. Sometimes the issue may be so petty that the couple discovers the fight was over nothing at all!

Listen

Discipline yourself to listen to as much of the details as possible before forming any opinions or making any judgements. Obtain understanding rather than jumping to a conclusion without the full picture. Be comfortable not saying anything and ask questions to encourage the superficial to lead into the deeper, hidden truths.

Respect

Attribute great value to your partner. Show respect. Do not criticise, swear at your partner, or call them names. Attack the problem and not the person. Focus on the issue. Expend your energies to resolving and not inflicting harm on your partner. If you must fight, then fight for the success of your relationship.

Be Mature

Act your age. Maintain composure and decorum. Have self-respect. Do not take your partner for granted or allow familiarity to breed contempt towards your partner. No tantrum-throwing, emotional meltdowns, ranting and raving or crocodile tears ought to be tolerated. Such conduct is immature, unbecoming in a healthy marriage, and has no benefit whatsoever to resolving conflict.

Exercise Wisdom

Men are generally physically stronger, have a deeper, louder voice due to bigger lung capacity, and are taller, heavier, and bigger in bone structure. When your head is hot with explosive steam, you may call it passion and emotion, but your wife may view you as Tyrannosaurus Rex, angry, aggressive, violent, and out of control. She may even see you as a candidate for an overnight stay at the police station.

Women can become hysterical, vicious, and just as guilty of physical violence and verbal abuse. Your point may be coming across sharp, cutting, and hurtful.

Therefore, in times of conflict, do what it takes to keep the perspective, exercise self-control, and avoid going berserk.

Have a Vision

Do you have a vision of 'the end'? Is it peaceful and harmonious with hugs and kisses? Or is it an end filled with anger, bitterness, and feelings of revenge? See the solution and not the problem. Aim for a good positive conclusion and work towards achieving it.

Discuss each other's expectations and test the reasonableness and workability; can you each satisfy the other's expectations? Otherwise, make the necessary adjustments or lower the bar. Remember to celebrate each other's attempts to serve the other.

Genuine Claim

"I'm working, doing all the housework, and paying for the mortgage and family expenses. I want to ask him to contribute but don't know how to. I fear that he may break up with me if I bring up the subject of money."

My Advice

Write down the issues and make it clear and to the point. Work out what amount of contribution is fair and acceptable to you. Then be courageous and request a discussion with your partner. Request that you both have an open mind and heart and avoid reacting or losing temper. Then discuss with gentleness and invite his comments while you suggest solutions and share the desired contribution amount.

Genuine Claim

"I suspect that my partner has mental issues. I do not wish to live under such conditions but don't know what I can do."

My Advice

This is a serious but common issue. You marry Mister or Missus Right, but after a few years, or perhaps a traumatic event, they seem to have morphed into someone completely different. Seek professional help from your local council, doctor or social worker. There are free services available for your partner to help diagnose and treat mental conditions. Persevering through this challenging time may prove rewarding, especially when you are both equipped with the right tools, therapy and sometimes medication. Even the most broken of relationships can be restored. Take heart!

MY SUGGESTIONS FOR YOUR ACTION

1. Make a list of your partner's characteristics and actions that you appreciate and are grateful for.

2. Make a list of your pet peeves and your partner's idiosyncrasies that trigger a negative emotion in you.

3. Share with your partner to resolve issues where necessary (limiting to one issue per sharing).

CHAPTER 8

UNDER THE SHEETS
~ SEXUAL INTIMACY ~

"Sexiness wears thin after a while, and beauty fades. But to be married to a man who makes you laugh every day, ah, now that's a real treat."
Joanne Woodward

I grew up in an era where sex was a taboo topic. Nowadays, thanks to movies, music and social media, the subject of sex is prolific and portrayed unashamedly. Some might even say we've gone too far! This evolution has been a fascinating journey to witness and discussing things of a carnal nature is no longer reserved for a doctor's visit alone, but a topic comfortably brought up by my friends and colleagues even while having lunch!

My marriage counselling work must involve the topic of S-E-X because sexual intimacy is a natural, intrinsic and important part of life and marriage. But before we pull back the sheets further on this topic, I must include a disclaimer that I have never, and will probably never, ever, hold myself out to be an expert!

Having said that, please enjoy the read ...

Amazing!

Sex ...

- Is the most amazing experience, signifying the physical union of two persons in the act of lovemaking, giving and receiving the deepest and best of intentions, being the highest spiritual ecstasy.

- Is shared preferably with someone you have committed to share your life with exclusively.

- Can be a great form of exercise, getting the heart pumping and the body burning approximately 180 calories for women and 240 calories for men, if each worked out in this manner for at least 60 minutes! (University of Montreal 2013).

- Is ultimately exciting, thrilling, and a lot of enjoyment and fun.

Because sex involves the greatest of intimacy and vulnerability, I would support reviving and heralding the 'ancient' beliefs that uphold the sanctity and purity of the marriage vows and keeping the marriage bed sanctified for one's partner. Sex ought not to be considered common and portrayed flippantly without respect and honour. It is special, significant, and honourable.

Purpose of Sex

Sex should be a natural consequence of a relationship that is built on love, enveloped in love, and flowing out of love. This act requires the union of two individual and separate persons becoming one. It is the ultimate expression of love between two persons who respect and trust each other, mutually desiring to give to the other through physical intercourse. There is greater pleasure in giving while simultaneously receiving, and this mental paradigm shift, even mildly understood, will transform one's sex life from self-gratification into the art of 'making love' to each other.

Envision two persons giving to the other out of selfless love, seeking to please the other, and in turn, experiencing the exhilaration and ecstasy of a very special meaningful union. Both persons will inevitably express themselves in so many ways through their body and soul.

The natural consequence of this physical union of love is procreation where precious tiny lives are conceived, and later, birthed and raised. Children are the fruit of sexual intimacy, the epitome of mystery and wonder, and the couple's legacy into the next generation.

On the flip side, when a couple cannot conceive and spend years trying, or investing in IVF or IUI, this can put stress on the sex life and pressure to conceive. The magic of the physical union and intimacy may suffer because of the pressure to 'perform'. Sex cannot just be about pro-creating. At the same time, many couples are terrified of falling pregnant, which can also have a negative impact on their sex life. If this is you, be wise and visit your health practitioner to get advice on birth control that works for you.

Factors that Destroy

Hurt and offences damage emotions and naturally negate the mood for sex. The proper way to restore intimacy is to humbly work through the circumstances that gave rise to the problem, apologise, and grant forgiveness. Otherwise, if quarrels persist, even after the pleasure of sexual activity, the hurt may cause one to feel hollow or unfulfilled.

A selfish person will not desire sex for reasons that lead to mutual pleasure. One ought to avoid using another person's body for one's own pleasure. Lovemaking is fulfilling when one selflessly gives to one's partner while simultaneously receives from the love of the other. Sex ought not to be used as a weapon to show one's superiority or to punish. Similarly, one ought not to withhold sex out of spite from unforgiveness or bitterness.

The following are some of the circumstances that led to the divorce cases I've represented:

- Ben was incredibly supportive of Pam working seven days per week as a medical practitioner. She earned a great income which allowed them to travel and provided the financial backing for his numerous business ventures (all of which failed). Sex wasn't prolific because she was usually fatigued from being overworked. Unfortunately, she wasn't able to have kids. Out of the blue, Ben asked for Pam's support to sponsor the visa application for a lady who worked as a maid in a faraway land, whom Ben had 'befriended,' and who had recently borne twins to him. He explained that this visa would enable the maid (and the twins) to live in Australia with them and that Pam's income would adequately support all five of them. Need I say that Pam was altogether shocked, numbed, and outraged, and that's how she sought my help to divorce Ben.

- Darren habitually put his wife down and chided her lousy cooking. He'd smack her whenever he felt that she wasn't performing to his standards. "It is our culture," he would say, despite everyone in that cultural community disapproving of his conduct. She tried to be the perfect wife even though she was tired after work and suffering from deep-seated hurt. After every sexual activity, she felt that her permission was forced, her will had been violated, and her body had been used.

- Lucy was so sweet to Watt whenever she wanted him to do something for her. But then during lovemaking, he felt she was frigid and unresponsive. This left him feeling frustrated and used. He eventually left her for another woman even though he claimed that he didn't stop loving her.

- Fred's wife enjoyed reading romance novels and watching racy adult content. When they made love, she would try to recreate the stories, but Fred felt that she was performing and imagining he was one of the men from her books. He gradually concluded that he was not good enough for her.

Proven Tips for Good Sex

I would like to share some time-proven tips for having good sex and maintaining good sexual relationships with your partner.

Tip 1 – Healthy Relationship Breeds Healthy Sex Life

Couples may start out with simple goals: We just want to be happy, to love each other, and spend the rest of our lives together. However, people are complicated, and good relationships take time, effort, and skill to nurture and mature. Conflict embers must be put out before they become bonfires. Offences must be resolved. "Make love, not war" was a popular slogan I heard a lot while growing up.

Marriage ought to be built on the foundation of love, good values, and great friendship, which is a perfect basis upon which for great romance and sex. If the marriage is built on sexual pleasure without nurturing the fundamental ingredients of a harmonious relationship, the marriage may not last. Quarrels and conflict can turn any sexy love bubble into a horror house of negative and unpleasant experiences. Magazines may make a fortune reporting on the love life of celebrities. Yet, the stories highlight the sad reality of a truth that may be difficult to swallow: Good sex may not equate to a good marriage. On the contrary, couples who consistently hold to good character and live by good values tend to be happy together and enjoy amazing sex.

Tip 2 – The Build Up

I have been told by sincere male friends that they think about sex 24/7 and they can be instantly ready to have sex. If this is true, then I categorically conclude that guys can multi-task, contrary to popular belief! If guys can focus on work or manage their daily routine while simultaneously being fixated on sex, then wow, guys are in fact masters at multi-tasking!

Xan shared with me that in his opinion, it was not possible for a guy to have a good friendship with a female and not end up in a sexual relationship with her. This is a fascinating concept to me and makes me wonder if this was the reason why ancient ones like King Solomon had 333 wives and 666 concubines during his lifetime. Mind you, this did not please the God he served!

For gals, on the other hand, sex is like a journey of happy moments with her partner, culminating with intimacy and ultimately, ecstasy and sexual fulfilment. In general, men must take their partners through a journey of stimulation and 'foreplay' that starts a few hours, or for some, days, before the sexual activity commences. Good companionship, joyful interactions, unexpected but inexpensive gifts, kind words, providing encouragement and support when the children are challenging her, noticing her hair, her dress, and showing genuine concern for how her day transpired – every little act of love adds up to prepare her psychologically, emotionally, and physically, for a beautiful time of intimacy together.

Neil learnt this and consciously exercised tender loving care towards his wife starting from Monday and throughout the week. By Friday evening, his wife was very ready to spend the night with him in pleasurable intimacy, and he was thrilled to have exponentially enhanced this aspect of his life.

Tip 3 – Sex Enhancers

1. Setting the ambience early through good communication, mutual understanding and harmony.
2. Stimulating mind and preparing heart for physical intimacy through love and tenderness.
3. Having fun experimenting before, during and after intercourse.
4. Being physically fit and flexible to accommodate all the variety of positions.
5. Being responsive to each other's likes and dislikes.
6. Obtaining education through books, videos, documentaries.
7. Having discussions with couples that you trust.

Tip 4 – Dispelling Myths

Myth 1 – I Need A Model's Body to Have Great Sex

Some are offended at their partner's physical imperfections. For example, a lady complained that in all her married life, her husband never once kissed her because he did not like the look of her teeth. In contrast, another lady's body was triple that of her skinny husband, but she didn't let her size hinder her confidence and knew how to please him sexually. They looked unlikely to be 'in love' yet had such satisfying sexual experiences which cancelled out any chance for extra-marital affairs.

It really doesn't matter if you have a spare tyre (also known as 'muffin top' or 'love handle,' which describes a large layer of skin around the waist), fleshy or bony bottom, too much or too little hair, too tall, short, big, small, round, flat. All these should not prevent parties from having great sex together.

Set realistic expectations to avoid misunderstandings and to ensure a truly pleasurable and memorable sexual life together. At the same time, you should try and be physically attractive to your partner. Just because they vowed to "love you for better or for worse" doesn't give you license to never go to the dentist or do a cardio session!

Myth 2 – No Talking During Sex

Hollywood has persuaded our perception of sex to be idealistically passionate, intense, steamy and thrilling. In a typical movie scene, there is no talking between the two, and only the sounds of gasping and the creaking bed.

This is contrary to reality! Sex can be awkward, messy, and highly technical. Couples ought to be talkative about what feels good, what does not work, which position is comfortable, etcetera. One needs to alert the other when feeling pain, when is it too rough or when more exertion is needed. Make sure you keep the noise down when the children are sleeping close by. Communication is necessary and ignoring what the movies portray is one key to enjoying great sex!

Myth 3 – Sex Must Last All Night Long

Is this true that sex must last all night long for it to be awesome? Well, for sure, if you can last throughout the night!

A 2005 survey of sex therapists (Corty & Guardiani 2005) produced these statistics about what people felt was the appropriate length of time for sex:

- 1 to 2 minutes – too short.
- 10 to 30 minutes – too long.
- 3 to 7 minutes – adequate.
- 7 to 13 minutes – desirable.

Excuse me?! Ten minutes was considered "too long"?! Therefore, avoid feeling pressured to perform any longer than that. Be realistic about the body's need to rest, especially after the rigours of work, parenting duties and other demands of the day. Be kind if s/he falls into a deep sleep immediately after, whereas you are re-energised. Be understanding and patient. You can always resume Part 2 on the next day!

Myth 4 – Foreplay Must Be Rough

If you are seeking to model your sex life after movie scenes of a sexy couple pushing and shoving each other around the furniture, pulling and ripping clothes off each other, buttons popping, underwear tearing, just remember that producers had a budget for replacing the damaged designer clothes! An alternative and preferable way for stimulation and arousal could be through loving words, removal of clothes with dignity, gentle exploring and showing consideration.

One of my friends, Han, loves to explore various foreplay methods. His top activity is dressing his wife's body with whipped cream and strawberries, then systematically licking and eating through the trail of 'dessert'. Eeew! I must admit that's a little too messy and sticky for my liking. Each to his and her own I suppose as it worked well for them.

Without getting too R-rated, the following are considered some pretty standard foreplay options:

- Roleplay
- Candles/good lighting/music
- Dancing
- Striptease
- Massage
- Sexy lingerie
- Kissing
- Showers/baths
- Dirty talk
- Toys
- Feeding each other food.

Myth 5 – Everyone Is an Expert

Many factors contribute to achieving a good sexual experience, including being conscious of the other party's feelings emotionally and physically and trying different positions and methods. It takes effort to find out what works and how to help the other feel pleasure. Trial and error, regular practice, and possessing a healthy sense of fun, will eventually lead to perfection. Not everyone is an expert at sex from the outset.

One of my friends, Arch, shared that he gave in to his girlfriend's advances but was inexperienced except for the guidance of having previously viewed movie scenes. Both of their expectations for explosive sex ended up in extreme disappointment. The sex turned out to be awkward, clumsy, unpleasant, and unglamorous. Being intoxicated and awaking to an unkind hangover afterwards accentuated how distasteful the whole experience had turned out to be.

Movies and videos are edited so that each scene is short, sharp and sweet. These are hardly positive guidelines for love that matures with time and flourishes from careful attention. The sexual union is delicate and meaningful and deserves the greatest of reverence. Getting proper education and gaining knowledge will be invaluable to assist in the exploration and experience. There is certainly no shame in being curious and learning about the G-spot, how to stimulate the other private parts, and the various important aspects of this subject matter.

Learn and grow together!

Myth 6 – The Morning After Is Perfect

Try to remember that movie directors choose actors who look gorgeous and attractive, and they awake looking pristine the next morning because it is staged. The reality may be waking up to bad breath, smeared mascara, a gaunt-looking face without makeup, and a grumpy disposition due to a caffeine low.

Don't be quickly turned off or discouraged. Simply let these all be incorporated into the colourful (and memorable) sexual experience!

Myth 7 – Other Inhibitors to Healthy Sex

Avoiding pornography because such a habit may feed on one's selfishness and isolation, which may impact negatively on the intimacy with one's partner. It can dehumanise and devalue the opposite sex to an object of lust, instead of upholding the intrinsic immeasurable value of one's partner out of love and respect.

A person may feel inhibited or extremely shy out of a conscious or subconscious constraint stemming from cultural or social influences or conditioning. For example, some cultures practise female genital mutilation, or girls are told that everything sexual is sinful, such that they grow up repressing the erotic side of themselves. Boys may have learnt that the female gender is only useful to satisfy their sexual needs, and this influences the flippant or careless way they treat their partners during intercourse.

Trauma such as rape can powerfully and negatively impact one's freedom to explore sexual intimacy.

Less than perfect parenting can impact upon one partner's trust of the other and prevent the emotional closeness that enables the sexual union to be more than just skin deep.

The marriage relationship can be a safe place of refuge and for healing, where partners can freely confide their deepest fears, insecurities, and past experiences with each other. They can also provide the comfort, tender care, and loving patience for the other to gradually become whole and free to explore and enjoy healthy sexual relationships together.

It does take two to tango, therefore create that refuge for each of you to feel safe to be vulnerable, to bare heart, soul, and body, then experience the ultimate feelings of being joined together as one.

Again, if problems persist, I'd recommend seeking professional help with a qualified sex therapist.

Genuine Claim

"I have a bad back and don't think I can have sex."

My Advice

There are many positions that will not harm your back. Be curious and explore new positions and methods. Remember to be gentle and to take things easy. Don't let the bad back stop you from enjoying this aspect of marriage with your partner.

Genuine Claim

"I'm pregnant and my belly is too big to have sex. I also don't want anything poking at my baby's head."

My Advice

You may be experiencing changes to your body, hormones, and moods. During the long period of pregnancy there are a myriad of activities you can do together as a couple that do not involve intercourse, while still satisfying your partner's sexual desire. Be creative. The love and intimacy need not sit on the back burner during the pregnancy.

Genuine Claim

"My culture and background do not allow me to enjoy sex."

My Advice

You are married and have formed a new household. This means that you can make new rules and set new boundaries. You can choose to disallow background, culture, or relatives from interfering with your marriage and how you enjoy the lovemaking.

MY SUGGESTIONS FOR YOUR ACTION

1. Discuss with your partner what actions encourage your desire for intimacy, and what actions dampens or quashes such desire.

2. Identify three problem areas that you can see to be having a negative impact on your lovemaking. For example, feeling unworthy, insecurity, cultural prejudices, inability to respond to touch, tiredness. Discuss together how to resolve these problems and work at overcoming these together. Be encouraging and supportive.

3. Make a list of ten activities you could enjoy together that does not involve sexual intercourse, but which will ultimately set the stage for a rewarding and pleasurable time of intimacy!

4. Find four new ways to enhance the variety. Allow creativity. For example, change the room lighting, explore new ideas together, or a different location other than the bed!

Additional Resources

Read *Everywoman* by Derrick Llewellyn-Jones (Llewellyn-Jones 2015).

CHAPTER 9

CRAFTING LEGACY
~ CHILDREN AND PARENTING ~

"There are only two lasting bequests that we can hope to give our children. One of these ... is roots, the other, wings. And they can only be grown, these roots and these wings, in the home."
Hodding Carter

My parents both worked in government jobs. Pa worked in the police force, and Mee was principal in high schools. They worked diligently to make ends meet. What strikes me is that no matter how long their working hours or how tired they were, they consistently prepared dinner for the family every weeknight comprising rice, three dishes (meat, fish, vegetables), and Cantonese soup stewed in the slow cooker from before we left the house in the morning. Mee's secret 'honey chicken' recipe was my number one favourite dish! I don't remember what we discussed during dinner, but I definitely cherish the memories of family dinners together. There are many benefits of having family dinners, and Kenny and I are committed to maintaining this tradition with our children!

The Right Ingredients

Babies are beautiful. They are a tremendous blessing and a great source of joy, overshadowing the numerous sacrifices that parents make, including sleepless nights, countless additional chores, financial commitments and much more.

From birth until about 25 years of age, every child's primary occupation is that of 'student'. There is much to learn and understand to become a well-rounded productive member of society. Parents must provide children with the crucial ingredients for nurture and growth including:

1. The *physical* fortress comprising:
    a. Necessities such as shelter, nutrition, clothing.
    b. A conducive environment for personal development.
2. The *emotional* casing filled with:
    a. Love, affection, comfort, security, support, encouragement.
    b. Positive relationships and experiences.
    c. Opportunities for learning about themselves and the surrounding environments.
3. The *moral* structure built on:
    a. Knowledge and wisdom.

  b. Teaching to know what is right and wrong.

  c. Training to choose the right over the wrong.

4. Activities, *fun* and play.

The best environment in which a child can blossom is one where parents shower their children with praise, love and encouragement, and teach them the right character and values and transfer important life skills.

Different Parenting Styles

It is the luck of the draw for children to grow up under one of the following smorgasbord of parenting styles:

- A laid back style where children are left to themselves without interference.
- Tyrannical parents who are overly controlling.
- Absentee parents who are away working or emotionally distant.
- Playful and careless.
- Serious and sombre.
- Dramatic, like how George Banks, in the classic movie *Father of the Bride* (Touchstone Pictures 1991), over-reacted out of his overly sensitive self-consciousness at almost every step of the journey from the time he received the news that his daughter was engaged right up to her wedding day.

It's not about which parenting style is right or wrong, but more importantly, that parents create a positive and conducive environment for children to grow and develop well. Children thrive on being loved, praised, encouraged, and taught well, the ropes of living successfully. These are ingredients that spur children on towards living beyond their limitations, to achieving the best results. And for this, they rely on their closest and biggest cheerleaders: mum and dad. Home must be a safe refuge for children to let their guard down, rest and refresh. Parents must give children time and space for this, or they will either lash out or become emotionally shutdown.

Whatever your parenting style may be, keep this end goal in mind: to give them roots for good grounding and wings to fly.

One's Parents Influences One's Parenting

From counselling young couples, I have observed that the parenting one receives as a child profoundly impacts upon one's adulthood, marriage relationship, and own parenting style. This fact can have positive or negative repercussions and ought to inspire our consciousness and diligence to acquire the knowledge and skills required to properly raise our children. Therefore, I wholeheartedly support couples' learning, reading, and attendance at courses, for the purpose of becoming successful parents.

Whereas some allow their personal insecurities to inhibit their leadership and parenting, others may inordinately focus on earning income and neglect the necessary involvement in disciplining and raising wholesome children. Often when parents complain about how stubborn or rebellious their children are turning out, the truth may reveal that beneath the visible superficial surface lies the invisible fundamental failure of parents to fulfil their parenting role appropriately. In other words, the children's bad behaviour is reflective of the parent's bad performance.

These client stories show where the problems originated, and how they were resolved.

Real-Life Stories	My Response
Andy felt resentful that his three teenage children daily waltzed in and out of the house without greeting him. They didn't acknowledge his faithful efforts to earn income to pay the mortgage, bills, and provide food for them. "They don't do any household chores. They want my provision but pretend I don't exist." He was angry, confused, depressed, and despairing.	I suggested that he ought to be the first to change and I gave him a list of homework to do. Firstly, he took the initiative and greeted each child cheerfully every morning. Secondly, he offered to drive the middle son to school and while together in the car, he asked about his studies, his aspirations, and how his siblings were fairing. Thirdly, he left post-it notes at strategic parts of the house with requests to do chores and purchase groceries. Six months later, his attitude towards his children changed. One year later, his children warmed up to him, and their relationship substantially improved.

Betty felt helpless that her two teenage children were starved of pocket money because their father (her ex-husband) had reneged on the financial support he had promised. She felt helpless not being able to purchase the iPads that her children needed for school.	I suggested that she could find a job to dispense with having to rely on her ex-husband. Further, her children could find casual work and find creative ways to earn an income, such as doing odd jobs for neighbors and selling things online. Initially, she baulked at the idea. It took some getting used to, but now they have three income sources supporting a self-reliant household.
Craig was charged with the criminal offence of theft. His parents were bewildered and felt it was "totally outside of his character." His parents removed his pocket money as punishment until the charges were dealt with at court (the process usually takes one year), hoping that "this will serve as the best lesson to help him change."	While taking instructions from Craig, I discovered that his pocket money amount was sufficient only for public transport. He didn't have any money to purchase food or other items that teenage boys fancied. I approached Craig's parents and persuaded them to be generous towards him, as more pocket money would prevent his becoming desperate and vulnerable to temptation, which was how he ended up getting into trouble with the police, after noticing and taking cash that was lying around unattended.

Parenting Team

Parents must be a team. Whether occupying similar or different roles, both parents must share the same values and objectives regarding raising children.

Many couples neglect the time and effort required to align their parenting philosophies. It is essential for parents to show a united stand as children have keen observatory powers to notice any contradictory standards and inconsistencies in decision-making. If children can push the boundaries, or play one parent against the other, they will do so. The risk exists that children will approach the 'right' parent for obtaining consent, knowing full well that the other parent was earlier disapproving. Furthermore, children may become conditioned to lie, manipulate, and be hypocritical, while adapting to parents who are not in agreement.

Leadership

Parents must take up the leadership in the family. Fathers must lead. Mothers must lead. Having a vision of the end will motivate parents to plan how to arrive at that destination.

Parents ought not to relegate the decision making to the whim and fancy of baby, child, or teenager. Children are added into the couple's relationship circle. They blend into the culture and life routine of the parents. Parents must not be afraid to lovingly confront the child who misbehaves, address the wrong attitudes and dish out parental orders or loss of privileges. Don't fall trap to letting the child take over and calling the shots. Every loud crying and tantrum-throwing in public, is not the cue for parents to panic and scramble to satisfy the child's whim and fancy. Rather, it is a fantastic opportunity for the parent to teach the child valuable traits such as obedience, delayed gratification, and contentment.

Even in wrongdoing, the adult must lead the way in humility and first apologise, then teach the lessons, call for reconciliation, and start the exercise of building trust and restoring peace with the child.

Children will feel secure when there is strong and positive parental leadership. Therefore, parents, strive to be an admirable leader, because one day, they will take the baton from you, and become parents of their own children. Paint the vision for the children to see what the future ought to look like when it comes time for them to leave the nest and make their own mark in the world through their parenting!

Discipline and Training

Parents are the primary teachers of their children, and this responsibility ought not to be abdicated to the babysitter, maid, childcare staff, or teachers. Although these individuals play a role in the children's upbringing, they cannot replace the parents' supreme position in their children's lives.

By being a good example to the children, parents can train children to learn the following well:

- Good character qualities => respect and honour for elders, courtesy, punctuality, responsibility, patience, endurance, integrity.

- Upright values => "yes" to hard work, honest income, justice, mercy, charity, and "no" to greed, accepting bribes, corruption, manipulation, power control.

- Financial acumen => wisdom in savings, expenditure, income, investments.

- Motor skills => practical skills such as ball handling, carpentry, handy work, handling fire.

- Emotional skills => ability to exercise self-control, resolve conflict, forgive, teamwork.

- Wisdom => choice of friends, discerning good from bad, decision making, foresight.

- Self-sufficiency => be self-motivated, negotiate purchases, obtain and maintain employment, run a business, raise a family.

Parents must teach and train their children. Don't wait to be given permission to speak into their lives. Instead, actively build bridges of trust and intimacy with your children, constantly share wisdom, provide counsel, and give instructions for right living. This is the foundational 'roots' that all children need from which to grow wings. Hence, if you can show them the right way of living, the values they would have learnt from you will remain with them for the rest of their lives.

Respect

Children deserve to be respected, irrespective of their age, whether baby or teenager, despite their size, gender, maturity and abilities. Each child is valuable, significant, unique, and beautiful. Embedded within their DNA is a special genius that is waiting to be discovered, developed, and nurtured, then released for productive contribution and the benefit of mankind. Therefore, parents should be guardians of each child. Be careful not to ignore, or demean, or act condescendingly towards them. Also, take care to avoid provoking, exasperating, or discouraging your children. Do not laugh at their mistakes. Don't cause them to suffer injury or harm by your actions towards them.

Parent's treatment of children at various stages of their growth will be different. Babies are helpless and completely dependent on you. Yet at that vulnerable age, babies are highly intelligent, aware, and responsive to you. When children grow up, parents must provide reasoning and explanations, rather than just instructing and dismissing any chatter and banter. As children transition into young adults, parents become counsellors and friends, and no longer 'dictators'.

Love

Love is the most important ingredient in parenting. Its positive effect can make a huge difference in children's lives. Parents can show love by touch, time spent with a child, giving presents, hugs, kisses, encouraging words and praises. Children flourish and blossom because of parental love and affection.

Employ the 'sandwich' principle to cushion any correction of your child. First the top layer with positive comments, then the middle layer where you share constructive criticism and feedback. Finally, finish up with the bottom layer full of encouragement. Alternatively, ensure only twenty percent of your time is spent teaching and pointing out mistakes. The other eighty percent of your efforts should be in loving conversation, heartfelt connections, eye contact and meaningful actions.

Making Time Count

Time does not stop ticking away. At a blink of the eye, children are grown up and leave home. Parents must be opportunistic and give top priority to investing wisely into their children, especially when they are available, receptive and responsive!

Be creative with the available time together. For example, cooking breakfast together, playing online games, building a treehouse, and gardening.

Dinner (or meals) together during the week is important. Make dinner times 'sacred' and say 'no' to any distractions, even good ones like work, sporting activities, television, and the smartphone. I'll be the first to admit my shortcoming here as a typical legal office day never seems to end before dinner time!

A survey of parents in 2019 (Anderer 2019) reported that sixty percent had dinner together, one-third sat in complete silence, and one-third discussed topics such as:

    a. Weekend plans.

    b. School gossip.

    c. The meal being eaten.

    d. Homework.

    e. Popular TV shows.

Another United Kingdom article (HealthLinkBC 2017) listed the following nutritional, health, social and mental benefits when families ate meals together:

- Great way to connect, have fun, learn about food safety.
- Children feel loved, safe and secure.
- Good time to teach family values and traditions.
- Learn how to say "no, thank you" to foods, or when they are full and need to stop.
- Develop healthier food habits.

Family togetherness provides a golden opportunity for connection and meaningful conversations about each other's lives. With everyone putting forward their best tips for living, the obvious results from these special times are positive outcomes for life. Children should be allowed to download and vent how they feel about school, homework, friends, and issues that they face. Be gentle and patient with them, even asking whether they want your advice before giving them an action plan.

A little time spent together regularly and consistently is more beneficial than a long engagement but only once in a blue moon.

Play

Children learn through play, and this holds true from babyhood all the way to adulthood. What a great life they have! Therefore, let children be cheeky, mischievous, and naughty. They are exploring, testing, stretching, creating adventures and memories for themselves. Playing allows children to use creativity and to develop their wild imaginations. Simultaneously, they exercise physical, emotional, and motor skills.

It is such a relief to know that parenting does not have to be solemn, grim, daunting, or overwhelming. Enjoy parenting your kids! Do fun things such as playing cards, board games, ball games, beach games, attending carnivals, camping, hiking, and trips away all benefit children greatly.

You Are Not Perfect

Be ready to admit that you are not perfect. Be humble and say 'sorry' when you've messed up. Children are usually forgiving and quick to wipe the slate clean. You don't have to have it all together.

You don't have to pretend to be strong when you are not. In fact, sometimes when parents appear unable to cope, children have room to exercise initiative, resourcefulness, and leadership.

My client Janet went through a divorce and had to fend for herself and her two young boys. As she struggled with the dual responsibilities of earning an income and running the household, both boys naturally rose to assist her with the challenges. Her elder by his own initiative found part-time employment to supplement the family income, and the younger became proficient at mathematics and accounting, assisting her with the family budget and payment of bills.

Latchkey Parenting

Lance works as a barrister. He shared with me that as a couple, they jointly decided that his wife would give up her career as a barrister and be the 'stay-at-home' mum. They didn't want 'latchkey' children who'd return to an empty home after school because both parents were at work.

Although alone time can encourage the children to become independent and engage in exploratory activity liberally without interruption from parents, there is less risk of children getting into trouble when parents are present, especially during the formative years.

If parents are emotionally unavailable towards their children, regularly respond impatiently or negatively towards their child who is trying to reach out for their love, this child may learn to suppress the natural desire to seek out a parent for comfort when in pain. The child may inevitably grow up to be cold, aloof, disengaged, self-absorbed, and even untrusting of their parents and others. They can become alien to relational concepts, after prolonged periods of feeling abandoned and rejected by or emotionally disconnected to their parents. (Catlett 2015)

Working parents or single parents must also spend time with their children and engage with them as much as possible. Lots of physical embraces, invite the child's interactions, celebrate the child's discoveries, welcome their sharing of feelings and thoughts. It's healthy even to allow the child to express frustration and other negative emotions, but afterwards, lovingly and gently guide them as to how to behave appropriately.

Parenting Through Negativity

As much as possible, children should be sheltered from unhealthy, negative experiences. Of course, there are situations where this is unavoidable, such as the death of a loved one or the family pet, and it's the parents' responsibility to counsel and guide children through these occasions of life.

Young children may not have the emotional resilience to cope with the trauma of parents quarrelling or incidents that attack their self-esteem and self-worth. Parents can say hurtful words and deeply offend children, without any such intentions to do so.

Children usually fly the coop after about two decades of living at home, or even later. Within that long period of time, a whole series of regrettable negative experiences can be accumulated. Children typically forgive and forget like water off a duck's back. But sometimes children may put up their defences to protect themselves from getting hurt. They can become passively aggressive or refuse to respond and keep silent. They may appear distant or disinterested.

Children need the support, understanding and skills to deal with and overcome negativity, and become whole again. After all, "it is easier to build strong children than to repair broken people." (Douglass 1855). If you sense a disconnect, give attention to repairing and restoring your child to wholeness. If necessary, obtain professional help from a school chaplain, family counsellor, psychologist, church pastor, or community, cultural or sporting group.

Genuine Claim

"My parents were not good parental role models for me while I was growing up. I don't know how to be a good parent."

My Advice

Your childhood experiences need not define you or dictate your present circumstances. Be at liberty to break the cycle of negative parenting passed down through the generations and create your own parenting style. Research what are the qualities of good parenting, then inculcate these into your best parenting ability!

Genuine Claim

"Because of the sufferings I endured as a child, I trip up when making decisions, and my lack of confidence inhibits my progress. I feel inadequate and a constant failure."

My Advice

Stir up the desire to conquer and overcome thoughts of self-sabotage and self-limiting beliefs. Work on healthy mental exercises to become strong and rid yourself of your shortcomings, weaknesses, and problems. Also, reach out to professionals who can assist you and keep you accountable for your growth and development. Invest in education and equip yourself with the parenting knowledge and skills to help you be a good parent.

Genuine Claim

"I failed at parenting, and the children are nearly all grown up. Is it too late to wish for good relationships with the children?"

My Advice

It is never too late. You did your best given the circumstances. Forgive yourself and put away blame and guilt. Start on a clean slate with your children. Explain to them your shortcomings and failures and ask for their forgiveness. Say something to the following effect: "I haven't been a good parent. I've read a great book on parenting and want to start afresh. Will you forgive me and give me a chance to set things right? I love you so much, and I want to hear your thoughts too." Together with your children, formulate a workable practical plan moving forward for healthy mutual communication, plan activities to do together like chores, gardening, carpentry. Living and doing together, and interacting and sharing, is a great start in the right direction.

MY SUGGESTIONS FOR YOUR ACTION

1. Listen to the lyrics of the *"Cat's In The Cradle"* song by Harry Chapin (Chapin 1974). Consider how this song could motivate you to spend time with your children, and what objectives you wish to achieve to better your relationship with them.

2. Capture the wonder that children bring to parents in *"The Greatest Love of All"* song by Michael Masser and sung by Whitney Houston (Masser & Creed 1977).

3. Watch the movie *"Despicable Me"* (Universal Pictures 2010) and observe how parenting three little girls gradually caused Gru to transform from supervillain into an unlikely but loving dad.

Additional Resources

1. Read *Making the Most of Childhood: The Importance of the Early Years* using this link: https://www.education.vic.gov.au/Documents/childhood/parents/mch/makingmostofchildhood.pdf (Victoria).

2. Read *The 5 Love Languages of Children* by Gary Chapman and Ross Campbell MD (Chapman & Campbell MD 1997).

3. Read *Boundaries with Kids* by Henry Cloud and John Townsend (Cloud & Townsend 1998).

CHAPTER 10

MEET THE KINSMEN
~ CONNECTING WITH THE IN-LAWS ~

"I got lucky: I love my in-laws."
Kaitlin Olson

It's a distant memory now because this occurred while I was growing up in Singapore, but I fondly remember the monthly gatherings at Grandma's which saw my mum and all her siblings attend dutifully with their families. She lived in a huge bungalow, and while my cousins and I played 'catching' and 'hide and seek' in the various rooms, the adults chattered about politics and current affairs. Grandma told me that she'd prepare a week in advance for this big feast, shopping for groceries during the week, and then spend the whole weekend cooking a storm of Asian dishes for at least twenty-five ravenous souls to feast on. This gargantuan effort emanated from her deep love for her family. For Pa, these in-laws were his family in Singapore since all his siblings lived in Malaysia. I missed this tradition after coming to Australia to study, especially because Grandma passed away shortly after I left Singapore. Nowadays everyone is too distant and too busy to gather in such a large and elaborate manner.

Extended Connections

Relationships are about being connected **to** other people and being connected **with** other people.

Couples not only commit to an exclusive long-term relationship with each other, but their union also involves being associated with at least *four* other people, who are the parents on both sides. If parents are re-partnered then potentially, that will be eight other people, or more if there are step siblings. Therefore, be prepared for an introduction to a new network of relationships within which to grow and flourish as a couple.

Sometimes conflict may arise due to a mismatch of personalities and perspectives. Be prepared to deal with issues to resolve misunderstandings. The objective is always to keep the peace and harmony and encourage good times and precious memories together. Blood is thicker than water, and these relationships should last a lifetime. Your married life will most certainly be enriched from these extended connections.

Blessings

It is important to nurture positive relationships with the in-laws. Grandparents can create the most beautiful and delightful memories for your children. Their involvement and input can be priceless! From helping children explore craft, teaching them how to bowl or read the stars, to expanding little people's horizons with each of Grandpa's stories, and filling empty tummies with Grandma's deliciously baked treats.

Your relatives will most likely want to spend time with you over meals, celebrating special occasions and other such activities. Therefore, be prepared to give priority to such social gatherings when you plan out your yearly calendar. It will be necessary to have a healthy balance to ensure attention is given to your inner circle (you and your partner) as well as to your outer circle (relatives).

Honour

There is an ancient edict exhorting children to honour their father and mother because it is accompanied by a promise of long life and peace (Moses 1980).

I grew up in the small island of Singapore where people were its primary resource, and the government's propaganda was designed to create harmony among its citizens. Filial piety, a Confucian virtue of honouring the elders in the family, was regularly broadcasted through the newspapers and television advertisements. Now, I'm not suggesting every person with grey hair is some type of Yoda that deserves our respect regardless of their past or virtue. But, in general, I do believe that we should respect our elders. Their great wisdom has been garnered through many years of life experience. Some have lived through world wars, economic upheaval, major changes in governments, and persevered through hardship and difficulty. Some have been involved in rebuilding the world that we now live in. We ought not to take for granted their sacrifices or dismiss the benefits of their wisdom.

Where possible, celebrate these precious relatives and set aside time to cultivate good friendships with them, no matter how busy or occupied you may be. The essence of honour is to attribute great value to these elders and even to enrich their lives with your presence and appreciation. In some cultures, youth are taught to show respect and reverence for elders by rising to their feet upon their entrance into a room or greet them by kissing their feet.

I urge you then, to have a humble and teachable attitude, and to be willing to glean treasures of wisdom from their insights. Esteem them highly and be patient during your interactions. You may be lively, quick, and agile of mind and foot. However, do not forget that these seniors may have been just as athletic in their heyday, but have now mellowed with age.

For the ones who may have grown up under abysmal parents, who are in jail, who are abusive, addicted to substances, and are plain terrible examples of how a good life ought to be lived, may I suggest that you keep your distance in order to protect yourself from the trauma and negative influences. Put on an adventuresome attitude and go out to find new parents to adopt. Find older couples or persons who are willing to be your 'parent,' to share life experiences together with you, be an example to you, and provide you with counsel and wisdom. In the same vein, there is always hope for the broken. I know many miraculous stories of terrible biological parents who years down the track, experience a transformation and become reconnected with their estranged family. But do proceed with caution. Love and respect must be mutually present.

Perks and Benefits

There can be loads of fun and benefits in integrating the in-laws and building meaningful relationships all around. As social beings, the wider the circle of relationships, the greater the benefits from the interactions and exposure to a variety of perspectives and unique personalities.

Everyone has skills and strengths that can be drawn upon to bless the greater whole. For example, one parent with handyman skills can assist with handiwork around the house. Another with baking skills will be welcomed at every family event! A retired parent who loves to spend time with grandchildren playing and teaching valuable life lessons will be perfect for babysitting duties. The most valuable benefit of having grandparents around grandchildren is the passing down of wisdom, stories, insights and tips for success that the older generation can share. One couple I know receives delivery of home-cooked meals each weeknight from their parents' kitchen! Such assistance and support can help to establish a young couple's marriage in its early stages.

Different Types of In-Laws

Working out the relationship with your partner is complicated. Adding the complexities of another two sets of parents, siblings and extended family may tip the scales either towards blissful happy living, or disaster. Obviously, I hope that the former rather than the latter applies to you!

Be aware that every family has its own unique idiosyncrasies, mindsets, and ways of doing things. Cultural differences can massively impact upon the differences in communication styles and behaviour patterns, and even provide grounds for conflict to arise. Latin Americans are known for being loud and passionate, which may appear overpowering in the presence of the British in-laws who may be quiet and reserved. Dutch people are often quite direct and may clash with Koreans who may be boisterous and rowdy.

My client, Dale, was confused and devastated that Zu's parents would pressure her to divorce him. He loved her and her parents to the best of his Australian ability, yet they refused to discuss the reasons for their many offences. My thoughts were that he was simply too Aussie for Zu's parents, who were simply too Japanese, and the cultures clashed. He spoke his mind and wore his heart on his sleeve, and this was too direct and forthright for their liking, as they were polite, gentle, discreet and would rather save face than speak the truth. The biggest losers out of this were their children.

Watch out for these differences in family types:

- Connectedness – very, somewhat, not at all.
- Time together – lots, little, nil.
- Telephone contact – calls, texts, daily, weekly, monthly, special occasions, nil.

Families manage conflict differently, for example:

- Meltdowns.
- Silent treatment.
- Passive-aggressive.
- Loud confrontations, then after all the issues are discussed, the people act as though nothing explosive had occurred.
- Negotiations.
- Formal meeting.
- Ignoring the conflict altogether.

What is your family like? How do they handle conflict or issues?

Families also handle celebration differently, such as the following:

- Organising parties for births, marriages, and festive occasions.

- Small quiet event with a meal and cake.
- Do nothing.

Friction

Some couples suffer from overbearing relatives who try to get involved without invitation. Couples ought to develop healthy values and establish clear boundaries so that they can peaceably manage their relationships with their relatives. Unfortunately, I have observed couples who were still in love go through with divorce because one of the partners was forced by the parents to choose parents over partner. Often, parents may feel that they have a right to help with the couple's decision making because, for example, they previously provided financial assistance to the couple to purchase their home. Sometimes, the parents' expectations are unnecessary or unrealistic.

My client Ruby was expected to help run the in-law's family business, cook, and clean, bear and raise children, without any acknowledgement or gratitude being shown to her. Another client came to me almost in tears, describing how his wife's parents had the run of the house, whereas he felt trapped in his own home and was constantly walking on eggshells wondering when his next movement or word would upset them and cause them to come down hard on him.

When the in-laws interfere in a couple's marriage, they can be intrusive or destructive, and if not managed properly, can weaken or negatively affect the couple's love for each other.

Success with The In-Laws

Relationships are complex. Making a permanent commitment to your partner may already be daunting and mixed with feelings of thrill and nervous energy from stepping out into the unknown and crafting the future together. Here are a few suggestions to aid your efforts towards building successful relationship with your in-laws.

New House, New Covering

Remember, once married, it is important for you both to come out from under the covering of your respective parents who were once your protectors, providers, and teachers. Whereas previously you were dependent on your parents for food, shelter, clothes, and finance, you must now step out to create your own household, have the liberty to create your own set of ground rules for decision making. Your parents now take the role of counsellors and friends.

The time has come for you to leave your parents and to be joined to your partner. Do not procrastinate or prolong the leaving. You must once-for-all cut the umbilical cord of connection with your parents. Break free so that you can start taking charge in your family. Cherish, care for, and protect your partner.

Mothers, one day you must let go of your son because he must assume his role as head of the house and leader of his family. Smothering your son or micro-managing his home affairs may not be beneficial. His wife's role ought to be respected and not usurped. Fathers, cease vetoing the decisions of your son (or son-in-law) or holding on to expectations that cause you to see him as not being 'up-to-scratch'. Let him make mistakes and learn, give him time to grow.

Boundaries

Start to create healthy boundaries early. How often do you want to visit your in-laws? Should they be allowed to discipline your children? Should they be consulted in decisions for the family? Do they have a say in how you save, invest and spend your money?

It is risky when couples cannot or don't know how to speak openly with their parents regarding boundaries, especially when the relationship is in its early and fragile stage. Ollie felt outnumbered when his wife sided with her parents in feeding their daughter traditional Italian food that was rich in flour and cheese, and as well as treats and lollies. Unfortunately, these were exacerbating the child's constipation and prolonging her suffering. His wife refused to speak up to avoid offending her parents. Ollie was angry that she was giving her family higher priority than their child's needs and welfare. He finally sought the help of professionals to introduce guidelines for the child's dietary requirements, gradually improving her overall health and well-being.

Aim to foster a connection with the in-laws while protecting and preserving the relationships through clearly-defined boundaries. Your couple relationship is the core circle of trust. The in-laws may be permitted into this circle or respectfully refused entry, according to your circumstances and at your discretion.

Expectations

Be fair and reasonable in your expectations of your parents. If you expect them to babysit your children while you are at the office, make sure to first check that they are willing and that it does not become a burden or obligation to them. Be considerate of *their* expectations, as they may have plans to relax, especially after many decades of working and raising children.

If you expect them to cook all your meals, be generous and offer to pay the costs of the meals, otherwise show your appreciation in other meaningful ways.

You may want to initiate discussions to discover what your parents expect of you and decide on a mutually satisfactory arrangement. For example, Elsie's parents visited her every year from overseas and expected her to host them and take extended time off from work to host their touring trips, at her cost. Eventually, the practical and financial strain on the family became too great to bear, after all, they had young children at school, she had a small business to run, and they were not financially well to do. After some discussion, her parents agreed to let Elsie do her thing, while they did their own thing. Her parents booked and paid for tours with agencies, which was unfamiliar but greatly beneficial because they ended up making many new friends during the trips.

Confrontation

Couples must not take each other's acquiescence for granted, nor imagine every circumstance will be automatically acceptable to the other. Communication is necessary if couples want to maintain harmony and peace in the marriage. Turning a blind eye or pretending nothing is amiss is not wise because the issue will remain unresolved and may one day blow up unexpectedly.

You can be kind and firm simultaneously. You can be truthful and direct, yet loving, in the confrontation. Your ability to address issues with your in-laws will be a good test of your loyalty first and foremost to your marriage. Many people are loyal to their parents at the expense of their marriage. This is not proper.

You must stay objective, keep calm, and exercise wisdom and maturity. Both must choose one's partner over one's parents.

Wives defend your husbands and stand up for him. Husbands shield your wives and speak up for her. Don't allow parents to denigrate or shame your partner, especially in the presence of children or anyone else. Break up any power struggle or arguments asap. Parents may mean well and have good intentions. However, if you have to choose between your partner or your parents, you ought to choose your partner!

Beware of the Money Lord

A few of my clients fell into quicksand when the parents of Wife had advanced funds for education or establishment of a business and used this ground as a bargaining chip against Husband. If Wife stood by Husband and tried to work out something reasonable with her parents, all would have ended well. Many matters involved my assisting clients to apply for divorce and negotiate a settlement of the couple's assets, because Wife had chosen her parents over her Husband.

My advice is not to allow money to be the deciding factor in your marriage.

Because the continual printing of paper money has put inflationary pressures on the value of goods, young couples are generally finding it difficult to purchase basic necessities such as the home, motor vehicles, even presents during Christmas and special events. Some couples rely on and welcome financial assistance from their parents. Granted, these are probably not the easiest topics to discuss, but it is important to clarify whether the money is a gift or a loan, whether interests applies, and whether there is a deadline for repayment.

Ernest's parents purchased a property in his name, for his residence during his tertiary education in Australia. He was confident of holding the title to the property on trust for his parents. They, however, insisted on putting an interest-free loan agreement in place to protect their equitable interest in the property. This action saved the property from being lost to Ernest's girlfriend, who after breaking up with him, tried to claim that she had a half share interest in the property for which she had not made any contribution towards.

Avoid Toxic Relationships

Unfortunately, some in-laws are impossible to be around. Watch out for the following:

- Constantly comparing you with others.
- Never-ending criticism about everything petty and insignificant.
- Conversations filled with negativity, dissatisfaction, and discontentment.
- Sowing seeds of discord and division.
- Stirring up arguments.
- Absence of love, joy, peace, and happiness.

These characteristics are unhealthy and not conducive to building up your relationship or allowing it to grow positively.

Some in-laws are manipulative and misbehave to get their way. Some use the grandchildren to pass messages to you. They may be seeking attention or have personal issues to deal with. Others may need money all the time, and you are their favourite banker! If possible, separate from the in-laws for a short period of time. Allow time to pass so that minds can reflect and change, forget, and hearts heal. Keep the distance so that you have space to focus on other things, gain new horizons and new visions for a better future.

Regardless, it will be necessary to deal with the situation and implement a smart strategy to regain harmony. Rid your circumstances of toxicity. If practical to do so, avoid toxic people altogether.

Genuine Claim

"My in-laws do not approve of me. I dislike having to go and visit them."

My Advice

There is not a lot you can do. They are entitled to their opinions and decisions. Nevertheless, you do not have to put up with their mentality. Ignore them or speak up for yourself. Explain your position. They may be blinded by prejudices and biases. If they persist in being negative towards you, limit your exposure to them.

The more important question is, how does your partner feel about this situation? Is he standing up for you? He must support you, encourage you, shield you, and build a strong marriage relationship with you, regardless of how your in-laws treat you.

Genuine Claim

"My parents do not approve of my choice of partner."

My Advice

To ensure marriage success, you must support your wife. You must be willing to step outside from under your parent's covering and start to build your own covering. You need to earn your own income, establish your own boundaries, and build your family. Be strong, take courage, breathe deeply, then go ahead and do whatever it takes to make your marriage succeed!

Work also to help your parents understand the reasons for your choices and the positive aspects of your partner. Unless of course they can see something that you cannot and are trying to give you forewarning. In that case, give them a listening ear, but discern whether their advice is noteworthy or of no value whatsoever.

Genuine Claim

"When my partner visits her parents at their home, she suddenly defaults into acting like a little child. Her parents fusses over her, and she becomes incapable of mature discussions. She defers to her parents' opinions on every subject. I am a little shocked and at a loss as to what to do."

My Advice

Find an appropriate time to gently confront your wife and let her know what you see. She may not realise and may be surprised to discover this truth about herself. Calmly explain what you expect of her instead. She ought to maintain her maturity and composure and avoid becoming a chameleon. In other words, she ought not to be acting maturely with you, and childishly with her parents. These habits are formed over time and may be entrenched. It will take a loving and observant partner to highlight the issue and keep the offending partner in check. Eventually, she may be sufficiently self-aware to catch herself and behave as she ought to.

MY SUGGESTIONS FOR YOUR ACTION

1. Reflect on your upbringing then share with your partner:
   a. What were your father and mother like?
   b. Identify what areas of your parents' personality you take after.
   c. Was your family discipline strict or relaxed?
   d. How were good grades and bad grades viewed?
   e. Did your parents celebrate you? How?
   f. Were your parents loving towards each other?
   g. How did your parents handle conflict?
2. Consider your internal family values together:
   a. What are your views towards parents transferring money to you?
   b. How will you handle a parent's behaviour that you may not approve of?

CHAPTER 11

HONEYMOON FOREVER
~ KEEPING THE RELATIONSHIP FUN AND FRESH ~

"In the words of my grandpa, a woman is as old as she looks, but a man is never old until he stops looking."
Iris Apfel

George and Sri are both retired doctors in their 60s. They asked me to prepare their wills, and we spent many sessions together brainstorming their requirements and how best to organise their estate. My first impression was how strained their relationship looked because she did all the talking, especially regarding death. He looked uncomfortable and kept silent throughout. She repeatedly stated her speculation that the minute she passes away, he would elope with a young Asian lady and take all the family's savings with him, leaving their six adult children high and dry. I was certain that she deeply distrusted him.

Gradually, George warmed up to me and started to share his stories. I was pleasantly surprised to learn that after 40 years of marriage, this couple's relationship was strong, full of humour and wit. The many cheeky remarks of death, infidelity and misappropriation of funds were jokes that arose out of their deep love for each other and sturdy friendship.

Another couple who are friends of mine are celebrating 60 years of marriage! Despite their quarrels and disagreements, their love has only grown and strengthened to the present day.

What are the secrets for keeping the relationship lively and fresh? Is it possible for couples to fall in love with each other over and again? Can couples enjoy a long life together? I would say a resounding "YES!"

Feeling Youthful

Everyone wants to remain young, even when the body, fitness level and agility diminish with each passing decade. To the 30-year-olds, the teenagers are babies. To the 40-year-olds, the 30s are young. To the 50-year-olds, the 40s are in the prime of life. In truth, 60-year-olds may have another forty years of living to do, despite energy levels not keeping up with their ambitions and new project ideas.

Reality of Life	Questions That Arise from This
Life may be routine, mundane, and full of pressure.	What to do to obtain relief and break the cycle of the same-old, same-old?
Busy schedules and unending demands to give out to everyone else may put out the fire and cause the relationship to grow cold.	What is the spark? Where do I find it? How can I keep the fire strong even during cold droughts?

Issues left unresolved or ignored may drive a wedge between the two persons.	How do I live through arguments, stalemate situations, exasperating events, and still be in love?
Long periods of neglect may cause the two persons to grow apart and become separate, even strangers.	How to support each other's individual uniqueness while allowing me to be me, yet making adjustments to keep the relationship harmonious, and allowing you to be you?

Let's explore whether the following seven suggestions may assist couples to maintain high energy levels, feel vibrant and inspired to continually enjoy the romance that sparked the relationship into life at the outset.

Celebrate

Have a balanced life, especially amidst the diverse range of responsibilities such as earning an income, managing the household, raising children, resting, celebrating, and having fun. Whether you are sanguine and naturally inclined to throw parties, celebrate birthdays and achievements, or introverted and phlegmatic, and prefer to avoid crowds, noise, or any type of activity requiring an adrenalin rush. Take my advice: celebration is necessary to keep one's marriage fresh and exciting, as air is to keep the lungs oxygenated and alive.

Don't miss the opportunities to acknowledge yourself or the people around you. Be kind, hand out gifts, or write a simple note of appreciation. Be creative and daring. Make it a regular habit to reserve a percentage of your income for celebrations; these may cost a lot or nothing at all. In my opinion, the only real cost is a bit of effort and time, and it may surprise you to know that the most memorable experiences are the ones that cost nothing at all.

When it comes to celebrating itself, let me introduce you to my friend Alexandria, who decided she didn't want to throw any parties for her birthdays. Instead, she splurged on herself as a reward for all her hard work in business and sacrifices for the family. For her thirtieth, she spent $200 to learn to sail. For her thirty-fifth, she purchased $1,000 worth of facial products. For her fortieth, she 'invested' $3,000 to live temporarily in a remote village in Thailand, teaching English to local students. For someone who didn't go shopping much, these birthday treats were significant moments of overwhelming joy for her.

There are so many reasons to celebrate, so don't let the big milestones or small pebbles pass by without an acknowledgement or a celebratory occasion.

For avidly frugal people, consider any expenditure on celebrations to be an investment into your marriage relationship. The benefits and returns are numerous, such as:

1. Counting one's blessings and reflecting on reasons to be grateful.

2. Expressing congratulations and appreciation creates a highly positive atmosphere.

3. Making time for each other brings a couple closer physically, mentally, and emotionally.

4. Sending messages of acknowledgement is a way to make deposits into each other's love banks.

5. Creating special memories marks important milestones in your relationship history.

6. Inject into your marriage with happiness and an energising booster.

Re-ignite the memory of your wedding day full of celebration, smiles, laughter, dancing, food, fun and extremely happy people. Now, imagine experiencing this positive adrenalin rush a few times each year, over small, medium, and large events, for all the right reasons. This is a great way to keep one's marriage lively and fresh!

A Sense of Humour

Be light-hearted. Be prepared to share jokes and positive comments. Develop your wit. Don't take yourself too seriously. Laugh at yourself. I've heard it said that a merry heart produces benefits like medicine! (Solomon 1980) I'm confident that laughter can repair and heal relationships. Try it on your partner today!

Joy acts like moisturiser on dried up relationships, smoothening out the wrinkles and removing tension from the atmosphere. It has a powerful ability to transform negative moods into positive ones. It can even recalibrate the direction of your marriage, from going downhill to cruising the airways.

Be careful to avoid coarse jesting, sarcasm, or being flippant and inconsiderate when expressing humour. Seek to edify and encourage, not injure or offend.

If you struggle with humour, watch some comedy films or professional comedians and learn from the pros! Drinking alcohol in moderation is a great relaxant and can help bring out your funny bone. Fred is a client of mine, who is a high-flying business tycoon and never lets his guard down. Once a week, he shares a bottle of champagne with his wife, and this transforms into a fun, light-hearted guy, and they have a wonderful romantic night. His wife later confided in me that she wished this 'fun guy' would come out more often. I'm not suggesting a bottle of champagne every night, but if you're particularly uptight, this may be a good way to unwind, even if it's only once a week.

Element of Surprise

At the outset, couples usually intend to live together forever. However, many may not be mentally prepared to live together, for say, up to 60 years, or even more! Because life is routine, it is easy to get discouraged with the following feelings:

- Going around in circles.
- Being caught in the rat race.
- Being stuck in a rut.
- Same old run of the mill.

Familiarity may breed contempt, and your once attractive partner may not be so attractive anymore. One may even be unmotivated for sex, which spells S.O.S and the need to call on the attention of emergency services! Take a moment out each day to be inquisitive, creative, and initiate something new. If you feel that you have no new story to share, I'd say it's high time for you to try something new and out of the ordinary. These are a few random suggestions for you:

- Write appreciative comments on post-it notes for your partner, then stick it on his lunch box, or on the bathroom mirror, for him to read.

- Give her gifts that she fancies and make spontaneous comments about her being a loving parent to the children.

- During meals with guests, pass compliments regarding his unique abilities.

- Give her a hug when she least expects or tickle her from behind.
- Take a few moments out of the daily kitchen chores and play 'aim the grapes into each other's mouths'.

Touch of Radical

Aim to experience something a tad radical. Do something that forces you out of your normal routine, out of your comfort zone, try something unfamiliar. Here are some random suggestions for you to pursue:

- Watch the sunset together. Drive to the beach or a viewing spot. Breathe deeply while staring into the vast expanse of the sky and sea. Do nothing but wait, soaking in the wonderment of nature. Smile and enjoy.
- Go cycling together and explore different routes.
- Train together to climb a famous mountain.
- Go canoeing or camping.
- Spend a day (or more) as tourists in your own town or country. Do as many activities as you can.
- Go for a ride on a horse-drawn carriage.
- Ride the Ferris wheel.
- Go to the theatre.
- Take a cocktail making class.
- Take dance lessons.
- Join a mission organisation to visit a local orphanage in a developing country.
- Visit a prison and assist with teaching life skills to prisoners.

Personal extraordinary experiences make for great conversation topics during family mealtimes or when visiting friends. These become the spark and refreshment that can inject life into your marriage. Do something that you would have never dreamed of doing. Don't overthink the costs or the risks. Don't procrastinate. Take the leap of faith and be forever changed by this great opportunity. Embrace the new challenges and let the adventure transform you. You will become better for it, and so will your marriage relationship.

Once I decided to go parasailing in Nepal. The cost was only AUD$50. But while I sat calmly throughout the hour-long drive up to the mountain, internally I was freaking out over a myriad of unanswerable questions running through my mind. I hadn't properly considered the reality of floating around in the sky without the security of metal casing. My will was not yet written up. I forgot to ring Kenny, who had remained in Australia, and it was too late to try because the wi-fi signal for mobile calls was non-existent at this geographical location and altitude. I had not given instructions for my memorial service. I was not sure if my life insurance covered extreme sports. Added to this, the feeling of overwhelming fear was new to me. I imagined my head falling off my body or crushing my short legs and toes while landing on the ground! I even changed my mind and asked the driver if he would let me out of the van and whether I could receive a refund of my money. Yes, I admit that for one whole hour, I had morbid thoughts, misbehaved, and asked many ridiculous questions of the driver and fellow passengers. I reckon I even managed to scare some of them to thinking twice alongside me! I was frantic and full of shaking on the inside.

But here's my parasailing story ... on hindsight.

- The jump off the mountain was really a walk into the air, natural, smooth, and uneventful. It took but one second from land to sky and I was suddenly soaring!

- The ride up high in the air was a-m-a-z-i-n-g and surreal.

- The experience was incredibly peaceful and beautiful. I felt safe in the harness and seat, with my guide behind and slightly above me.

- I had a clear and uninhibited vision of the whole sky and earth below. I had bird's eye view of many parts of the landscape below that one normally would not and could not see – rice fields, goats grazing on the mountainside, roads meandering through green and brown landscape.

- Given the chance, I would go parasailing a hundred more times.

- The ride turned out to be too short after all and I was sorry it was suddenly over.

Keep Learning and Growing

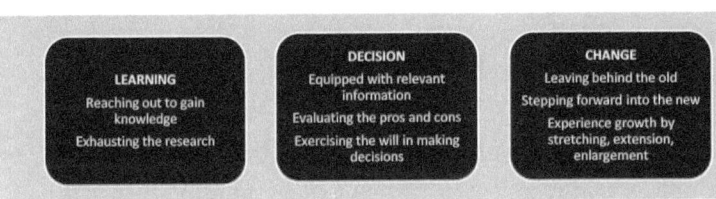

The human life is intended for the constancy of learnings and dynamic growth. Self-development is essential for individual health and vitality. So long as you have breath in you, you ought to be continually learning new things and growing. This will help your relationship to stay fresh. Therefore, couples ought never to think that they have arrived at some conclusive end, but rather, understand the many benefits of embracing change, such as the following:

1. Changes usually make people more broad-minded and big-hearted, which brings satisfaction and fulfilment.

2. Change is accompanied by inspiration, and this positive energy is contagious across all areas of life.

3. Change kills boredom.

4. Change stretches individuals out of their cocoon and evolves them into a new person, who is progressive, fresh and filled with joy.

Reimagine Retirement

Couples should reconsider retirement because being continually productive while serving others with one's abilities may be the secret to the greatest fulfilment in life! Business tycoon, Warren Buffet, who does not believe in retirement, was eighty-five when he said this about working: "You'll have a more interesting time, and you'll remain more engaged than if you spend your time watching the world from your back porch." (Zetlin 2016)

When we were about thirty, Kenny and I formed this grand plan to be financially able to retire at forty. I have since changed my mind and decided that working is good for my health. Kenny, however, has been planning to retire for the last two decades, and with every passing year, he gives himself another five years to retire. Every year, I have a good laugh at his expense, because he absolutely loves his job and I cannot foresee him ever retiring.

You could use your 'retirement' years to:

- Write a book to capture your wisdom, skills and share experiences gained through life.
- Mentor the younger generation of entrepreneurs.
- Coach a sporting team.
- Pursue the hobby that was put on the back burner.
- Or just relax!

Cultivate Meaningful Friendships

I agree wholeheartedly with the phrase "one's network is a show of one's net worth" but in more than just financial ways. Being around people who are positive, growth-oriented, wholesome and fun-loving, can have the biggest and best impact on your marriage relationship. Healthy friendships can lead to all the following:

- A new perspective on life given by someone totally unlike you.
- Enriching interactions over meals while exchanging life stories that inspire, spark new ideas, and challenge your status quo.
- Synergy from the mutual contribution of gifts, talents, skills and expertise that could lead to new business ventures and community projects.
- Opportunities to share challenging times and receive the encouragement, comfort or support.

Genuine Claim

"I cannot wake up in the morning. I have no energy after work. I can't even think of wanting to do anything new."

My Advice

You may be suffering from fatigue and lack motivation. Evaluate your state of health and fitness, your diet, and your sleep patterns. You may need to change your daily routine to include exercising three times per week for at least thirty minutes each. Include more fruit, vegetables, and supplements into your diet. Insufficient nutrients can lead to sluggishness, loss of energy and bad moods. See your doctor for a general health check. Also, spend time and effort discovering what will spark vitality in your life and marriage.

Genuine Claim

"My partner is negative. Everything to her is impossible. There are far too many risks. She has reasons to shoot down every new idea."

My Advice

There is nothing wrong with pursuing an activity without your partner. She is a different personality, and you cannot force her to become the same as you, and neither can she force you to become like her. Therefore, go after your exploits alone, and later return to share the story with her. Encourage her to do the same. Recognise your respective uniqueness, support each other's quests, celebrate by telling and hearing each other's stories. Hopefully, after your partner sees you enjoying life and hearing all your great stories, she might even be tempted to join you.

Genuine Claim

"We have been so busy that we have lost track of all our friendships."

My Advice

Response: Make a list of the people that you previously had connections with. Systematically contact each person or couple. Put in the effort to meet up. Organise activities for the families to bond. Rebuild the friendships.

MY SUGGESTIONS FOR YOUR ACTION

1. Reflect on your top three 'wow' experiences with your partner. Include details of the dates, venues, occasions, the smells, colours and who else participated. Then talk about it together.

2. Create a vision board of all the things you would like to experience or learn to do that you have not yet had the opportunity.

3. Make a list of two activities you would like to try in the next year. Work out the cost, the time needed, and all the arrangements for you to make it work, despite your work and family schedules.

CHAPTER 12

THE SEASONS OF LOVE
~ LIFE'S DIFFERENT PHASES ~

*"To everything there is a season,
a time for every purpose under heaven."*
King Solomon

Original Design

The original design for marriages is "till death do us part." Such relationships are intended to last forever, and I'm confident that the majority who marry truly believe that their relationships will last forever.

Relationships usually blossom through romance, exude vibrancy and love, and the general perception is that it looks perfect and promising. The evolving nature of the relationship goes through different stages, seasons, and many experiences. It would be wonderful for these traits to remain and for the love never to stagnate, become stale, or grow cold.

Throughout this book, I have shared tips for navigating through the journey of married life. Hopefully, these will inspire you, encourage mental preparation and give you confidence to work towards a fulfilling, successful, and long future together.

The Key of Preparedness

I wonder if couples are aware that their marriages will journey through different seasons, and whether they are mentally prepared to embrace and overcome the challenges that accompany the different seasons. Some people commit to marriage and expect to cruise through to success. Without the basic skills of communication and conflict resolution, people can be shocked by the apparent irreconcilable differences that may lead to an inevitable breakdown.

Whereas some seasons may be filled with spontaneous adventure and fun, other seasons may be wrought with pressures and stresses, or feelings of emptiness and depression, or even loss or sufferings or hopelessness. There are lessons to be gained in every season of life, and I encourage couples to regularly reflect to observe the bigger picture and overall circumstances. There will be plenty of reasons to be thankful and grateful in each season of life, whatever the experience may be.

Below is a discussion of four seasons in any relationship. Later, I suggest tips that could be guiding factors for you to draw upon throughout the many seasons of your relationship.

Spring Season

The birth stage of the relationship – excitement.

This is a time of great discovery which includes many happy 'first-time' experiences, such as the following:

- The first meeting.
- The first signs of attraction.
- The first date.
- The first kiss.
- The first time she meets my parents.
- The first time he meets my friends.
- The first daytrip we take together.
- The first home-cooked meal together.

It also involves spending time loving each other through fun activities and discovering each other's heart, attitudes, thoughts, and charms.

Spring is also the time of establishing the structure for the relationship. If you want to build a big house, your foundation must be sufficiently deep and strong. Before putting up frames and bricks, the wise will spend the necessary effort to ensure the foundations are right.

Imagine two individuals who have been independent and self-supportive. Once married, they must become inter-dependent, co-operative, selfless and generous for the successful marriage. Decisions to be agreed upon include solving the balance of power, working out what roles each will assume in the household and who will look after the day-to-day finances. Will one parent remain home to nurture the children, or will the children go to childcare?

During this season, the love between the couple overwhelmingly forgives idiosyncrasies and pet peeves. Conflict is quickly resolved. It is easy to make up after a quarrel.

Summer Season

The stage of baby-making and raising children.

Clucky couples have massive fun making babies, which a wise friend of mine claims is the easy part. Raising children, however, takes a lifetime of effort, but is extremely fulfilling and worth all the blood sweat and tears.

Parents run from errand to errand, looking after the baby 24/7, who is totally dependent, helpless, and with little ability of its own. It blissfully enjoys the simple life of eating, playing, pooping and sleeping. The parents, by contrast, have responsibilities of employment, mortgage, car repayments, accumulating savings and investing for future returns, and teaching and equipping children.

Children progress through to primary school and high school, which increases the burden on the parents. This includes planning, transport, after-school sport, music and academic tuition. The objective is to train up the best well rounded human heroes, ready to take on the world.

Couples usually imagine what life will look like at retirement and put in the effort to build a retirement nest. This means saving and investing funds into income-producing assets, whether property or liquid assets such as shares, managed funds, bonds, term deposits etcetera.

This period of life is commonly characterised by an immense amount of energy, strength, drive and passion. There are many activities and responsibilities to juggle. Those feeling tired and drained must maintain a good diet, exercise, and supplement with vitamins and minerals. This should give turbo-boosted performance and support for this season.

I caution couples to focus their abilities towards building the family, their income and resolving conflict with grace and patience. Couple time, family holidays and social connections will enhance and enrich the marriage during this time.

There are so many aspects to this phase of the marriage, which makes it vulnerable to earthquakes and cracks. Couples must be mindful to preserve and guard the relationship for strengthening rather than allow love to wane into disrepair.

Autumn Season

Ideally, the couple ought to move from survival to overflow phase, having established the home and savings after a few decades. Their children may have completed education and have started an apprenticeship or found gainful employment. Now is an opportune time to explore hobbies and holidays, undertake community services. Freedom to enjoy each other's company away from the pressures of work and family. Some people embrace a new career entirely or enrol in higher education.

Winter Season

Fondly known as 'the empty nest' stage of marriage, where the adult children are independent, have wheels, are married off. You may be wondering, "What do I do with myself?" Though in some cultures, there is no such thing as retirement.

I encourage you to explore and be open to fresh new adventures. Attend the University of the 3rd Age, learn to paint or support a local church in its activities. Mentor the next generation, give back to the community. This is the experience of one of my friends who had a positive, unassuming attitude. After the passing of her precious husband with whom she shared 40 years, she took hold of life with both horns. She has formed many new friendships and accumulated many stories of her travel experiences. She is an accomplished painter and hosts many church activities in her home.

Further Tips for Marriage Success

If you want to achieve success in marriage, you must imagine training for and running a marathon. The journey is long, and the qualities of perseverance, endurance and long-suffering are the magic carpet on which you must ride. Here are a few guiding principles to assist your journey.

Rules For a Happy Marriage (Author Unknown)

1. Never both be angry at the same time.
2. Never yell at each other unless the house is on fire.
3. If one of you must win an argument, let it be your spouse.
4. If you must criticise, do it lovingly.
5. Never bring up mistakes from the past.

6. Neglect the whole world rather than each other.

7. Never go to sleep with an argument unsettled.

8. At least once a day say a kind word or pay a compliment to your partner.

9. When you have done something wrong, admit it and ask for forgiveness.

10. It takes two to make a quarrel, and the one in the wrong is usually the one who does the most talking.

Commitment

Love is a commitment to build a two-way relationship that will stand the test of time. It is not a sprint that draws its life from short bursts of energy and thrills. The marriage vows are meant to be fulfilled by each party. The consistent application of underlying values and principles in every situation will help the relationship survive through storms.

Practise Good Values and Principles

Your marriage mantra should simply be these three things:

1. Love
2. Respect
3. Forgiveness

Put it up on the wall as a daily reminder.

Teamwork

Work together.

If there is any need for attack, attack the problem and not each other. Aim to solve amicably.

Discover what characterises a good team player and perfect these qualities in yourself.

Be the strength to cover each other's weaknesses.

Discipline the children together with the objective of teaching them the best way of life.

Defend each other against the children, the in-laws, even friends. To any accusation against your partner, say, "that is uncharacteristic of my partner," and then sort it out with him/her privately.

Love is not automatic. One cannot take for granted that love will remain constant throughout the seasons. Often one must make deposits into the love bank and exercise sacrificial effort.

Just like investing in shares, one must invest time and effort to become educated with how to trade on the stock market. The trading must be constant over time, to ensure the shares are growing in value. If attention is not given and the shares are forgotten, one may miss the opportune time to sell and capture the gain in value. They may also miss the opportunity to purchase at a good price. Building your marriage (and your children) requires constant monitoring, evaluating, good decision making, and investments.

Long Distance Relationships

Couples can still grow closer, stronger, and build deep and meaningful relationships, even if the relationship is long-distance. This may be due to employment, business, education abroad or military service and could be over a long or short period. Proper and regular communication is the key. Organising gifts to be sent to your partner via online purchase will create special memories. When you spend time together on the weekends, days off, or during annual leave, keep some intimate alone space for yourselves.

Working Long Hours

We live to work. Work is good for our health. It fuels motivation, breeds intention, and the sense of accomplishment and reward is fulfilling. Couples, however, must guard against any imbalance of working long hours at the expense of their couple and family time. Urgent and important work may inevitably require long after hours. However, this ought not to develop into the norm. Remind yourself to rest, refresh, and consistently invest in your marriage, even in the requirements of work.

Roving Eyes, Rolling Hearts

Be loyal. Do not get distracted. Temptations can be very deceiving. The fling is temporary. The instant gratification is short-lived and leaves one unsatisfied. The quest for more can become an addiction that leads one on a long road away from love.

In my time, I have observed wives who were faithful and committed, who looked after the home and children while their husbands worked overtime or overseas, wake up overnight to discover that hubby had been having an affair with the secretary, the business partner, the music director, or the patient.

Gentlemen, watch out for female vultures lurking around you and watching; they have generous amounts of time and energy to plot the flirtatious abduction of you out of your marriage. They seek to boost your ego and seduce you with gifts and flattering words.

Ladies, beware of self-interested guys who are searching for a thrill, a warm body, a refuge in a relationship that may be idealistic to them, but devoid of any consideration of benefit to you.

Remember your vows and commitment to your partner and the ultimate reward after working through hurdles and challenges. Living with your chosen companion and closest confidant till your old age is of greater worth than chucking it all out for a one-night stand.

Weigh it up. Would you give away everything you have built for a fling? Or stick it out for the long haul? The grass is not always greener on the other side of the fence, especially when the work has not yet been completed on this side.

A UK law firm reported in 2018 that 22% of the participants it surveyed regretted ending their marriage (Seddons 2018).

Relationships are complex because people are complex. Whereas I herald loyalty and longevity, there may be a myriad of circumstances that warrant otherwise. Yet, after extensive investigations into the theories, research, and therapy surrounding extramarital affairs, some experts have found that marriages can survive affairs and even grow stronger (Zur PHD n.d.)

Thinking about Quitting

People consider quitting for a variety of reasons. One party may be negative, abusive, is addicted to substances, or be hot-tempered. These can cause injury to the relationship.

Sometimes, one is stubborn and refuses to change, and may not welcome counsel. A couple may be unequally yoked with different objectives. They will both be pulling in opposite directions.

Before you throw in the towel, may I urge you to give it another shot, but agree to try something brand new. Sit down together and discuss the issues. Try to compromise and agree on how to move forward. Guard your marriage from breakage. Fight to keep your marriage. Aim for victory and success.

Grant wanted advice on separation and division of assets. He felt the relationship had ended due to his wife's hard-nosed attitude towards everything, especially money. After a few sessions with his counsellor, he confronted her, they both worked to resolve problematic issues together. Their marriage is now restored, and there is harmony between them.

Looking for a Fresh Start

If you are looking for a partner, try searching online dating websites or applications of good repute. Research reviews, horror stories posted, dangers and costs associated with these as well. It's best to research which site is right for you. Some are considered hook-up apps connecting people for casual sex. Whereas others are geared towards helping couples establish permanent relationships. A few may cater solely for people aged over 50.

You can enlist the help of friends with a good command of English and a creative flair for advertising to help craft your profile and evaluate prospects.

It's important to know what you want in your prospective partner. Make your requirements clear, then qualify your prospects before meeting and pursuing any relationship. This will help you to avoid being distracted by persons who are not suitable for you, or who are not genuine.

Be cautious of sexual predators or confidence tricksters who are solely seeking to benefit from and prey on young, naïve, or vulnerable people who are genuinely focused on finding 'true' love.

Maggie was swept off her feet by a guy she'd met through an online dating website. They shared numerous electronic messages together. His work as an investment banker greatly impressed her, especially when he claimed to be from Switzerland but was working temporarily in Australia. She did not suspect his 'inability' to communicate via video. He showed her a picture of a diamond ring worth AUD$20,000 and asked her to be his fiancé. He sent her an electronic copy of a certificate stating her ownership of USD$1 million worth of shares. He asked her to lend him AUD$10,000, which funds she borrowed, then agreed to drive one hour into country Victoria to hand over the cash to a stranger acting as his agent. He managed to persuade her to purchase a property in preparation for their life together. As I worked on her property conveyance, I uncovered the truth of this elaborate and spurious scheme. I had to break the news to her that the only authentic parts of this relationship were the money she gave away, and the property she purchased, for which she had absolutely no means to settle.

Winston was captivated by photographs of a voluptuous and beautiful lady, and he couldn't resist her incessant persuasions of him to lend her money. "It's to help my business get afloat," she claimed. After sending her AUD$5,000 over two transfers, he sought my objective advice, which was a simple two-liner:

"RUN for your life" + "she has zero love for you."

Can you believe that I had to repeat the second part of my advice to Winston several times over just to convince him? It wasn't an easy exercise, and I had to work hard to earn my fee!

Ditch the Baggage

Be free from baggage accumulated from your upbringing or from past relationships. Resolve internal issues within yourself, be as whole and healed as possible in preparation to meet your new partner.

Look out for someone who is similarly whole. One of my clients who had not resolved her hurts from childhood met a dashing lad who also had unresolved issues from past relationships. Try as they may, they could not make the relationship work or last for very long. Their insecurities caused them to distrust each other. They were fearful of any form of commitment and failed to achieve anything more than skin deep connection.

Genuine Claim

"We have grown apart. We are holding on to the relationship for the sake of other people. But in truth, we have nothing in common."

My Advice

Go back to the start when you were both in love. Try to find your store of love letters and gifts to each other. Relive the excitement. Spark to life the love you first had for each other. It is possible to take baby steps in the right direction to revive and restore your first love. Then fan the tiny flame into a bonfire. Do not give up!

Genuine Claim

"I am feeling depressed about an accident I have suffered, which has left me handicapped. I feel hopeless, unattractive and lost."

My Advice

I have met several people who worked hard to rehabilitate and have managed to turn their circumstances around from helplessness and hopelessness, into a fulfilled life with an income-generating career.

John was hit by a truck while cycling and became paralysed. He lost everything. Out of sheer willpower he taught himself to read and write and exercised his limbs to full mobility. When I met him at a conference, he had already qualified to provide professional services to clients for a good fee.

Peter was given the wrong anaesthetic, which left him paralysed and bedridden. He willed himself to full health, obtained a post-doctorate degree and now earns a living prescribing alternative medicine for people's ailments.

Robert was riding his motorbike when a ute ran into him. He should have died. Today he has completed a degree in computer science and is training to compete in the Paralympic athletics event at the Commonwealth Games.

Do not sell yourself short. The world is your oyster, and the opportunities are endless, so long as you are determined and willing to work. Have a go at redefining your future.

Genuine Claim

"I made a mistake with gambling and lost everything. I cannot face my spouse. I am too ashamed to continue living."

My Advice

Forgive yourself. Ask for your spouse's forgiveness.

I met Andrew, who had been homeless for six months. During the nights, he slept in front of the iconic Flinders Street Station in Melbourne. On one of his taxi trips, he had a chat with the taxi driver, which changed his life completely. Today, he is a property developer and owns six properties.

You must allow yourself to dream, to venture out and embrace opportunities. Do not be afraid to pick up the pieces and try again.

MY SUGGESTIONS FOR YOUR ACTION

1. Identify what season you are in now.
2. Evaluate the following together:
    a. Who is better at decision making?
    b. Who is fastidious, who is easy-going with tidiness?
    c. Who is exact with punctuality, who is laid back?
3. Share with each other, feelings and thoughts regarding the goals, successes, and regrets of each season of life.

AFTERWORD

Please accept my heartiest congratulations for arriving at the conclusion of this book. Bravo! Yee-har! I hope you took the long route and read all the chapters in their entirety and didn't take any short cuts.

I also hope that you will make this book a good resource and staple reading throughout your marriage, one that will live on your bookshelf as a regular reference to be used when specific chapters become relevant to your circumstances.

Perhaps you know of couples who are struggling or even ones just embarking on marriage. This could be a great tool that you can give to them for the secrets and tips on nurturing happy, harmonious and long-lasting marriages.

May the principles herein support your relationship to withstand the trials and weather life's storms. Just as you embarked on the marriage journey gloriously, may you also sail through to a glorious finish.

I welcome your stories, feedback and comments, and any questions that you may have. I'm sure these will be of great assistance for the sequel!

WORKS CITED

Anderer, John. 2019. "Dinner & No Conversation: Third of Families Sit in Silence While Eating, Shock Survey Reveals." *www.studyfinds.org.* 13 September. https://www.studyfinds.org/dinner-no-conversation-third-of-families-sit-in-silence-while-eating-shock-survey-reveals/.

Carstensen, Laura. 2015. "Why Should We Look Forward To Getting Older." *Ted Radio Host.* 19 June. http://www.npr.org/transcripts/414999589.

2004. *The Notebook.* Directed by Nick Cassavetes.

Catlett, Joyce. 2015. "Avoidant Attachment: Understanding Insecure Avoidant Attachment ." *PsychAlive psychology for everyday life.* https://www.healthlinkbc.ca/healthy-eating/eating-together.

Chapin, Harry & Sandra. 1974. *Cat's in the Cradle.* Performed by Elektra.

Chapman & Campbell MD, Gary & Ross. 1997. *The 5 Love Languages of Children.* Chicago: Northfield Publishing.

Chapman, Gary. 1992. *The Five Love Languages: How to Express Heartfelt Commitment to Your Mate.* USA: Northfield Publishing.

Cloud & Townsend, Dr Henry & Dr John. 1998. *The 5 Love Languages of Children.* Australia: McPherson's Printing Group.

Cloud & Townsend, Henry & John. 2003. *Boundaries in Marriage.* Maryborough Victoria: Zondervan Publishing House.

Corty & Guardiani, Eric W. & Jenay M. 2005. "Canadian and American Sex Therapists' Perceptions of Normal and Abnormal Ejaculatory Latencies: How Long Should Intercourse Last?" *Volume 5 Issue 5 Pages 1251-1256.* USA: The Behrend College, May. 1251-1256.

Douglass, Frederick. 1855.

2002. *My Big Fat Greek Wedding*. Directed by Joel Zwick. Performed by Gold Circle Films.

Goldstein, Jessica. 2014. *Kaitlin Olson on Her New Girl Guest Role, It's Always Sunny Season 10, and Why Drinking and Acting Don't Mix*. USA: New York Vulture Chat Room.

Gray, John. 1992. *Men Are From Mars, Women Are From Venus*. USA: Harper Collins.

HealthLinkBC. 2017. "The Benefits of Eating Together For Children and Families." *HealthLinkBC British Columbia*. https://www.healthlinkbc.ca/healthy-eating/eating-together.

Hepburn, Katharine. 1996. *Me: Stories of My Life*. USA: Ballantine Books.

Hodding, Carter. 1953. *When Main Street Meets the River*. University of Michigan USA: Rinehart.

Jessen, Kyle. 2013. *Dancing in the Rain: Life Isn't About Waiting for the Storms to Pass*. USA: Westbow Press.

Keen, Sam. 1999. *To Love and Be Loved*. USA: Bantam Books.

Lapin, Rabbi Daniel. 2014. *Business Secrets from the Bible: Spiritual Success Strategies for Financial Abundance*. USA: John Wiley & Sons.

Llewellyn-Jones, Derrck. 2015. *Everywoman*. Great Britain: Penguin Books.

2014. *Iris*. Directed by Albert Maysles. Performed by Magnolia Pictures.

Masser & Creed, Michael & Linda. 1977. *The Greatest Love of All*. Performed by Arista.

Moses. 1980. "The Holy Bible, New King James Version." *Deuteronomy 5:16*. USA: Thomas Nelson Inc.

Qoheleth. 1980. "The Holy Bible, New King James Version." *Ecclesiastes 3:1*. Thomas Nelson Inc.

Seddons. 2018. *2016 Financial Settlement Divorce Survey*. Survey, UK: Huffpost.

Silberberg, Fred. 2016. "11 Marriage Truths from Divorce Attorneys." *Huffpost*. https://www.huffingtonpost.com.au/entry/marriage-truths-from-divorce-attorneys_n_56cf434ae4b03260bf75d3ed.

Solomon, King. 1980. "The Holy Bible, New King James Version." *Proverbs 17:22*. Thomas Nelson Inc.

Works Cited

1991. *Father of the Bride.* Directed by Charles Shyer. Performed by Touchstone Pictures.

1997. *As Good as it Gets.* Directed by James L. Brooks. Performed by TriStar Pictures.

2010. *Despicable Me.* Directed by Pierre & Chris Coffin & Renaud. Performed by Universal Pictures.

University of Montreal. 2013. *PLOS ONE.* https://www.menshealth.com/sex-women/a19537023/sex-workout/.

Victoria State Government Department of Education and Training. 2017. *www.education.vic.gov.au.* August. https://www.education.vic.gov.au/Documents/childhood/parents/mch/makingmostofchildhood.pdf.

Weaver, Fawn. 2013. *Till Death Do Us Part.* http://www.happywivesclub.com/till-death-do-us-part/.

Wilde, Oscar. 2015. "Oscar Wilde The Dover Reader." *Courier Dover Publications* 460.

Woodward, Joanne. 2016. "Iconic couples sharing declarations of love." *Hello!* 8 February. https://ca.hellomagazine.com/celebrities/02016020823050/iconic-couples-sharing-declarations-of-love/10/.

Zetlin, Minda. 2016. *3 Reasons Warren Buffett Says You Should Never Retire.* 14 January. https://www.inc.com/minda-zetlin/why-warren-buffett-says-hell-never-retire-and-you-shouldnt-either.html.

Zur PHD, Ofer. n.d. "www.zurinstitute.com." *Infidelity & Affairs: Facts, Myths and What Works.* http://www.zurinstitute.com/infidelity/.

ACKNOWLEDGEMENTS

This book is the cumulative efforts of so many people who encouraged, assisted, critiqued, and added their brush strokes behind the scenes to help me throughout this inaugural author process. The true list bears many more names all of whom I am extremely grateful, but notably *Steven Teo* who in 2014 watered the innate seed within to author books, *Sarah Lim* for holding me accountable until I crossed the finish line, *Anne and David Butler* for refining my Singlish expressions, *Linda Long* for your refreshing perspectives at each juncture, *Fiona Ku* for the purple sticky notes, *Annabelle Teo* for personifying the many visions of this book during a grand milestone juncture in your life, *John Sikkema* you speared new challenges for me to overcome, *Jessica Whitehill* for pushing me to the 9.9, the many membered *Ultimate Denman Team* for holding my hand throughout this journey (especially for the memorialised 'social butterfly' award), and all the *August 2019 Retreat Authors* for inspiring me with your stories and successes.

To *Kenny, Daniel* and *Joshua*, thank you for being so generous and gracious in allowing me the freedom and the absence to embark on this.

You all share in the successes of this book and the positive impressions indelibly marked on, as I'd hope, a great many lives.

JOYCE KHOO

Joyce Khoo wears several hats.

As a Lawyer she has worked on divorce matters for more than two decades resolving disputes over property and children and observed the many dynamics of healthy and broken relationships.

As a Christian Pastor and Marriage Celebrant over the last decade, she counsels couples in Relationship Enrichment and Preparation (REAP) and has married a few.

As a wife for almost 3 decades, she experienced it all, the romance, blissful happiness, tensions, struggles, mud fights, sparring matches, through dealing with the usual issues of children, pets, chores, money, in-laws. Her choice of forbearance over dissension and the constant efforts made to resolving all sorts of differences has been the key to harmony despite obvious differences in personalities and other aspects of life.

As author of *Harmony for Couples: A Divorce Lawyer's Ultimate Guide to Marriage Success* Joyce shares her insights to the building blocks for couples to achieve success and longevity in their relationships. She sees the success in every relationship and can help couples to achieve it!

Joyce's best 3 philosophies for couples to achieve success in relationships:

1. Develop the best communication abilities
2. Be skilled at resolving conflict
3. Mix fun and laughter into the rigours of one's relationship

Joyce's best 3 preparation advice:

1. Don't rush the process in building a good foundation for the relationship
2. Agree on your values
3. Just keep learning and growing

Joyce is available for speaking engagements and REAP.

Contact Joyce Khoo and visit www.joycekhoo.com today.

NOTES

www.ingramcontent.com/pod-product-compliance
Lightning Source LLC
Chambersburg PA
CBHW021832110526
R18278200001B/R182782PG44588CBX00006B/7